Hulton New Histories

1. TRIBES AND TRIBUNES

(from earliest times to A.D. 410)

Philip A. Sauvain

Contents

1. Hunters and gatherers

The first peoples

Look at this photograph. It shows the trunk of a great tree which once grew in northern England about 250 million years ago. We can see the tree today, because luckily its shape and appearance have been preserved in sand. Perhaps it was buried in a sandstorm in about 250 000 000 B.C. In the millions of years since then, that sand has gradually hardened into sandstone.

● What is the name given to a plant or animal which has been preserved in stone like this?

The stone tree was formed at about the same time as the coal which can be found in many parts of Great Britain. At that time there were many unusual animals in Britain, such as dinosaurs. There were also many different plants. But there were no human beings.

Experts think the first humans lived about 1½ to 2 million years ago. You can see people like this in the picture at the top of the opposite page. They probably used sticks and stones as tools. They had no skill at making tools and weapons of their own. They lived by eating seeds and fruits, not by chewing meat.

● Which types of animals did these people look like?
● Were they carnivores (meat-eaters), herbivores (plant-eaters) or omnivores (creatures which eat both plants and meat)? Which of these are you?

No-one can be absolutely certain that peo-

Stone tree at Stanhope, County Durham

ple like these were the ancestors of the human race. The descendants of the people shown in the picture may have later died out and become extinct. We may be descended from other creatures whose remains have not yet been discovered. What we know about the early history of the human race has to be pieced together from discoveries, such as bones and stone tools.

Neanderthal people

Tools, weapons and animal bones which are about 100 000 years old tell us about a group of humans who lived in the Neanderthal valley in Germany. These humans were much more advanced then the ape-like people who lived about 1½ to 2 million years ago. The Neanderthal people ate seeds and fruits, but they also hunted animals for their meat. They made simple tools by chipping pieces off flints so that these could be held in the hand and used as simple knives or hand axes.

Other prehistoric peoples with a similar way of life are also called Neanderthal people, even though they lived a long distance away from the Neanderthal valley.

● In what ways were the people who lived about 20 000 years ago (seen in the lower picture) even more advanced than the Neanderthal people? Make a list of the differences you can see between the two pictures.

1 500 000 years ago

100 000 years ago

20 000 years ago

History skill: making a time-chart

Historians often show what happened in the past in a diagram called a time-chart. Different periods of time (like the Stone Age) or actual years (like 1984) are listed in order of time. This is called chronological order. It means that the earliest date is shown first and the most recent date last.

Other columns in the time-chart are put alongside. You can then see at a glance when famous people lived, when important battles were fought, or when new inventions were discovered.

Part of a time-chart, using the information in the pictures on these pages, is shown below. Copy this time-chart and then complete it after studying the pictures

Time-chart: early peoples

When they lived	Food	Tools and weapons	Other facts
1 500 000 years ago	Ate	Used	Lived in groups and families for protection.
100 000 years ago	Ate	Used	Knew how to keep a fire alight.
20 000 years ago	Ate meat from animals as well as seeds and fruits	Used	Knew . . . .

stone hand-axe
40 000 years ago

**Stone Age tools found
at Creswell Crags**

flint point

flint blad.

30 000
years ago

flint point

flint point

12 000 years ago

The Stone Age

It is hard to imagine that the people seen in this photograph are walking towards a cave which was once the haunt of hyenas in prehistoric times. We know this because hyena bones have been found here in Derbyshire. Bones of the bison and the wild horse have also been found. The cave was home at different times for several groups of prehistoric peoples.

Over 40 000 years ago, a tribe of Neanderthal people, like those you can see on page 3, lived in these caves at Creswell Crags. We can tell this because they left behind primitive hand-axes. These were roughly shaped from pebbles found in the area. These axes are typical of those used by Neanderthal people in other parts of Europe.

Ten thousand years or so passed and then the caves at Creswell Crags were inhabited again. A new group of people came to live here who were much more advanced in their way of life. We know this because the tools

they left behind are longer, narrower and sharper than those which had been made by the Neanderthal people.

The Creswellian people

Another long period of about 15 000 years passed and then yet another group of people lived in these caves. They too were hunters.

• How do you think archaeologists know that these people (who are known as the Creswellian people) also lived in these caves and that they hunted horses?
• Why do you think archaeologists call them the Creswellian people?

The Creswellian people had much better stone tools than those of any of the earlier cave peoples. You can see some of their tools in the picture above.

• What tool is shown in the drawing at the bottom on the extreme right? What do you think it was made of? What could they make with this tool? What does this tell you about the Creswellian people?

Creswellian people about 12 000 years ago

Animals in the Stone Age

One of the most famous discoveries at Creswell Crags was of a bone decorated with a carving of a horse's head. It had been carved with a sharp point made from flint. Another carving showed a human being and another had an attractive zig-zag pattern.

Animal bones found at Creswell Crags included those of the cave lion, wolf, bear and woolly rhinoceros. Animals like these lived at different times in the Stone Age. When the weather was cold, animals with warm coats, like the mammoth (a type of elephant) and the woolly rhinoceros, were able to survive. When the weather got warmer, animals used to hotter climates took their place.

• Why is this long period of time known as the Stone Age? What was made from stone? Why weren't metals used then?
• See if you can find out whether any Stone Age tools and implements have been discovered in your home area. A guide book to your district or a local-history book may give you this information. You will almost certainly be able to find out if you visit your local museum.

History skill: looking for clues

The tools used by people in the Stone Age, their carvings and cave paintings and the bones of the animals they hunted are clues. They help us to build up a picture of everyday life in prehistoric times.

Write two or three sentences to say how the clues in the list below helped the artist to draw the imaginary picture on this page. All these finds were made as the result of excavations at Creswell Crags.

— a bone needle;
— a flint scraper with a sharp edge;
— a carving of a horse on a piece of bone:
— a spearhead;
— a burnt animal bone;
— animal bones and bird bones.

2. How we know about prehistoric times

Archaeology

Imagine you have moved to a new home with a garden. You help dig over a rough piece of waste ground at the bottom of the garden. To your amazement you discover:

— two rows of bricks about 2 metres apart;
— many fragments of glass;
— one or two pieces of very coarse pottery, reddish brown in colour;
— a blackened coin dated 1971 and another coin dated 1959;
— a piece of charred wood;
— a tin box containing a handful of seeds.

● What type of building have you discovered? What can you say about it? What happened to it? When was the last date when you can be reasonably sure it was still standing?

Archaeologists find out about the distant past from similar discoveries to these. The discoveries are the hidden clues which help them to work out how people lived thousands of years ago. The finding of a piece of jewellery may tell them that people liked to dress up. A mirror may indicate that they took a pride in their appearance. An arrowhead shows that they knew how to use a bow and arrow, even though the bowstring, wooden bow and wooden arrows have long since rotted away.

Archaeological sites

Some of the places where archaeologists dig have been found by accident, Mechanical diggers or bulldozers sometimes unearth pottery when preparing the foundations for a

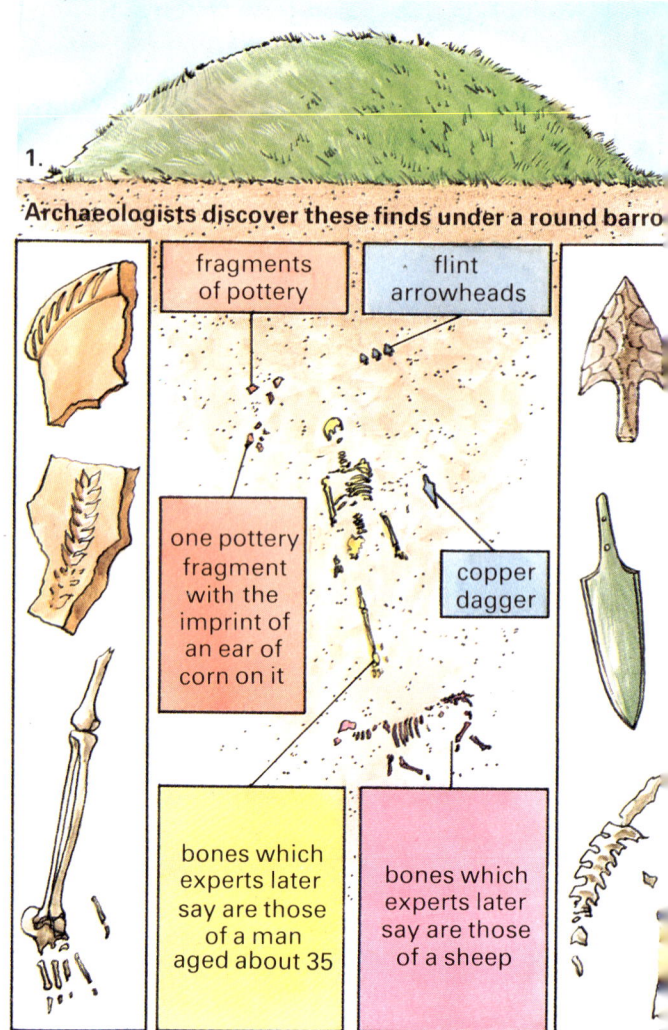

1. Archaeologists discover these finds under a round barrow

fragments of pottery

flint arrowheads

one pottery fragment with the imprint of an ear of corn on it

copper dagger

bones which experts later say are those of a man aged about 35

bones which experts later say are those of a sheep

building. Other sites are excavated (carefully dug) because the archaeologists can see that the land has been raised into mounds which are thought to have been the work of prehistoric people.

You can picture the way that archaeologists work if you look at the plan on this page.

2. They piece together what they think may have happened about 3600 years ago

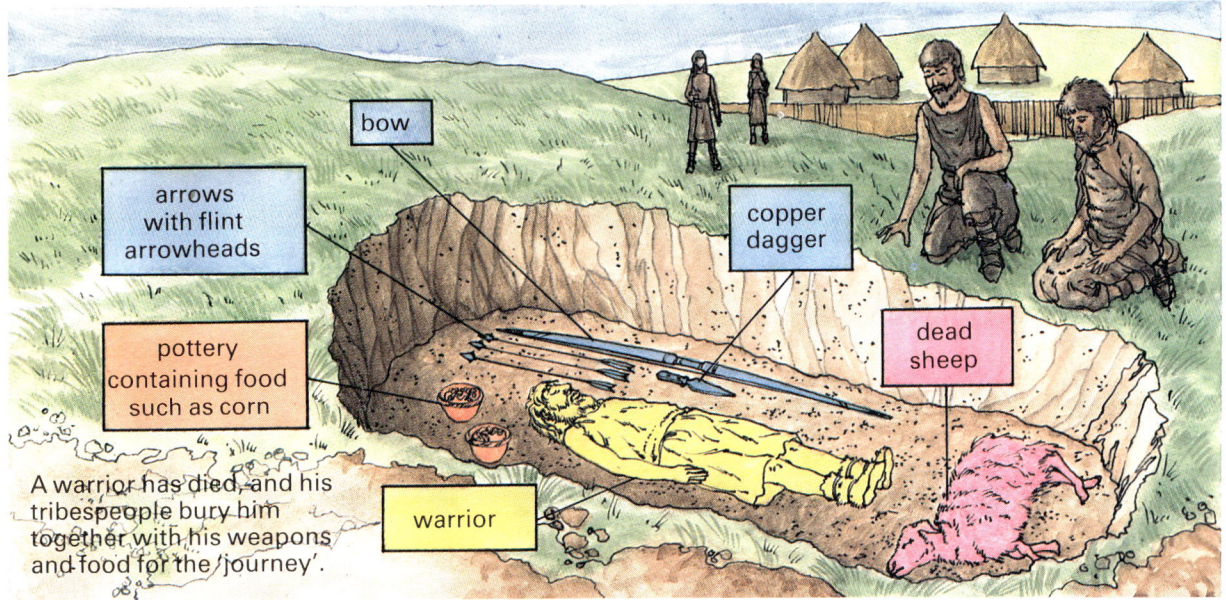

bow

arrows with flint arrowheads

copper dagger

pottery containing food such as corn

dead sheep

A warrior has died, and his tribespeople bury him together with his weapons and food for the 'journey'.

warrior

These are the sort of remains which might be discovered under a type of prehistoric mound, called a round barrow. Archaeologists know from previous excavations of round barrows that it probably contains the remains of a warrior chief who lived about 3600 years ago.

Evidence
Finds like this are sometimes called evidence. Just as evidence is given in a law court to prove someone guilty or innocent, so evidence is used by archaeologists and historians to show how people lived in the past.

History skill: using evidence
Look closely at the different finds shown on the plan. Make a list of them and then write against each the things it tells you about life 3600 years ago. Compare your list with the picture on this page. This shows how the artist has used the same clues to picture what may have happened when the warrior chief was buried 3600 years ago.

Look at the evidence found under the round barrow and answer these questions.
1. Was the warrior a young man or an old man? How can you tell?
2. How do you know he was a warrior? How was he armed?
3. How do you know the people who lived in this village were probably farmers? What did they produce?
4. How do you know these people were more advanced than those who lived during the Stone Age? What stone tools did they still use?
5. How do you know these people had some form of religion and thought about questions such as life and death?
6. Why were a dead sheep and a pot filled with corn placed in the grave?
7. Write a few sentences to say what the finds in the round barrow tell you about the everyday life of the people who lived in this area at that time. Here are a few sub-headings to help you with your work: FARMING, TOOLS, WEAPONS, BELIEFS, MATERIALS.

Imagine it is the year A.D. 5000 and that a team of archaeologists is busy excavating the site where your school now stands.
Draw up a list of the *ten* most useful discoveries you think such a team could make to help them build up an accurate picture of life in your school at the end of the twentieth century.

Dating the past

● How would you try to find out how old these objects are:

— a newspaper yellowed with age?
— a well-worn coin?
— an old photograph, showing women in long dresses?

You might find these tasks quite easy, since the coin and newspaper would probably have dates on them anyway. You could easily find out from a book when women wore long dresses like those in the photograph. It would be much more difficult if you were given a piece of prehistoric pottery or a flint tool. Even trained archaeologists sometimes have difficulty. They need to know exactly how and where an object has been found.

Excavations

At an excavation, archaeologists expect to find the most recent objects near the top and the oldest finds near the bottom.

● Why do they expect this?

As you probably know, the remains of many old buildings lie buried under the ground. You can imagine what happens if you look at the picture diagram below.

Four thousand years ago, some Stone Age farmers build a small village of thatched huts. They don't intend to stay there long. After a time they take their herds of cattle and flocks of sheep to other pasture lands some distance away. The huts start to collapse and weeds begin to grow among the debris. Discarded clothes, rubbish and straw thatch decay. Many other things which would tell us about their everyday life begin to rot.

Gradually soil blown by the wind, or washed there by rain, covers the site. The last remains of the village are buried. Luckily for us some of these remains, such as pottery and flint tools, do not decay quickly. But they lie underground.

Hundreds of years later, deep layers of soil cover the site. Then, about 1500 years after the first village was abandoned, a new village is erected by Iron Age farmers. They are called this because they have iron tools and a much more advanced way of life than that of the Stone Age farmers.

What archaeologists may find during an excavation

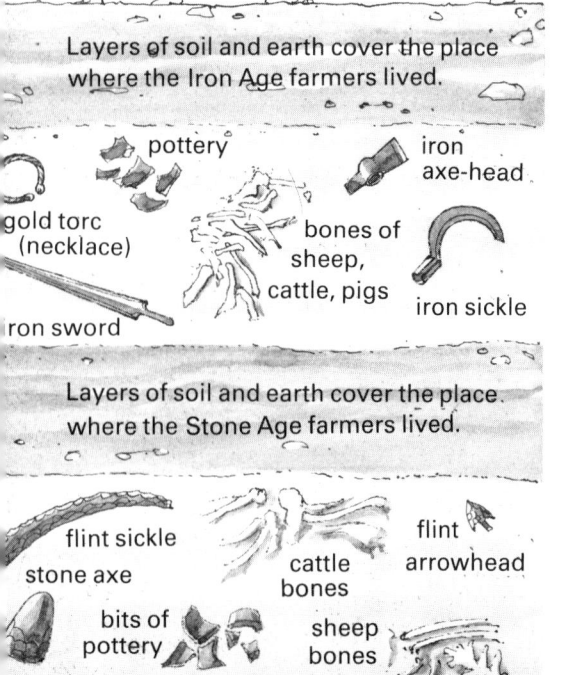

Layers of soil and earth cover the place where the Iron Age farmers lived.

pottery

iron axe-head

gold torc (necklace)

bones of sheep, cattle, pigs

iron sickle

iron sword

Layers of soil and earth cover the place where the Stone Age farmers lived.

flint sickle

stone axe

cattle bones

flint arrowhead

bits of pottery

sheep bones

The history of the area

today

about 2500 years ago

site abandoned

Iron Age farmers plough small fields with iron ploughs, and grow corn. They clear trees with iron axes. They keep sheep, cattle, pigs.

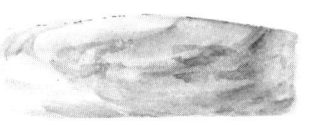

site abandoned

about 4000 years ago

Stone Age farmers dig fields with flint digging sticks and harvest corn with flint sickles. They also hunt with bows and arrows.

But several hundred years later their village too is abandoned. The remains of their homes and their way of life lie buried beneath layers of soil and earth.

- Which remains would a team of archaeologists discover first of all if they excavated this site?
- How would they know that the flint sickle and fragments of pottery found close by were made by the same people, and at about the same time, as the stone axe and the flint arrowhead?

History skill: dating the past

Look carefully at these diagrams. They show imaginary excavations in three different places (or sites).
1. Did the Stone Age hunters live before or after the Stone Age farmers?
2. Did the Bronze Age farmers live before or after the Iron Age farmers?
3. Did the Bronze Age farmers live before or after the Stone Age farmers?
4. Put the four groups of people in order of age. Name the oldest group of people first and the most recent group of people last.

- How do archaeologists know the Iron Age farmers were more advanced than the Stone Age farmers in the ways in which they:

1. harvested their corn?
2. cleared woodland?
3. defended themselves?

How does this sort of knowledge also help archaeologists to say how old something is?

Prehistoric peoples
The Stone Age farmers did not know how to smelt or work metals. However, they were more advanced than the Stone Age hunters because they grew crops and reared animals. They didn't have to hunt for all the food they ate, although they still collected wild seeds and fruits and hunted wild animals.

The Bronze Age farmers knew how to smelt copper and tin and how to mix them together to make bronze. This is a tougher metal than either tin or copper. But they didn't know how to smelt iron. The Iron Age farmers knew this secret and were able to use iron for weapons and sharp tools. Iron is very strong and can be sharpened to make a fine cutting edge.

The results of three excavations

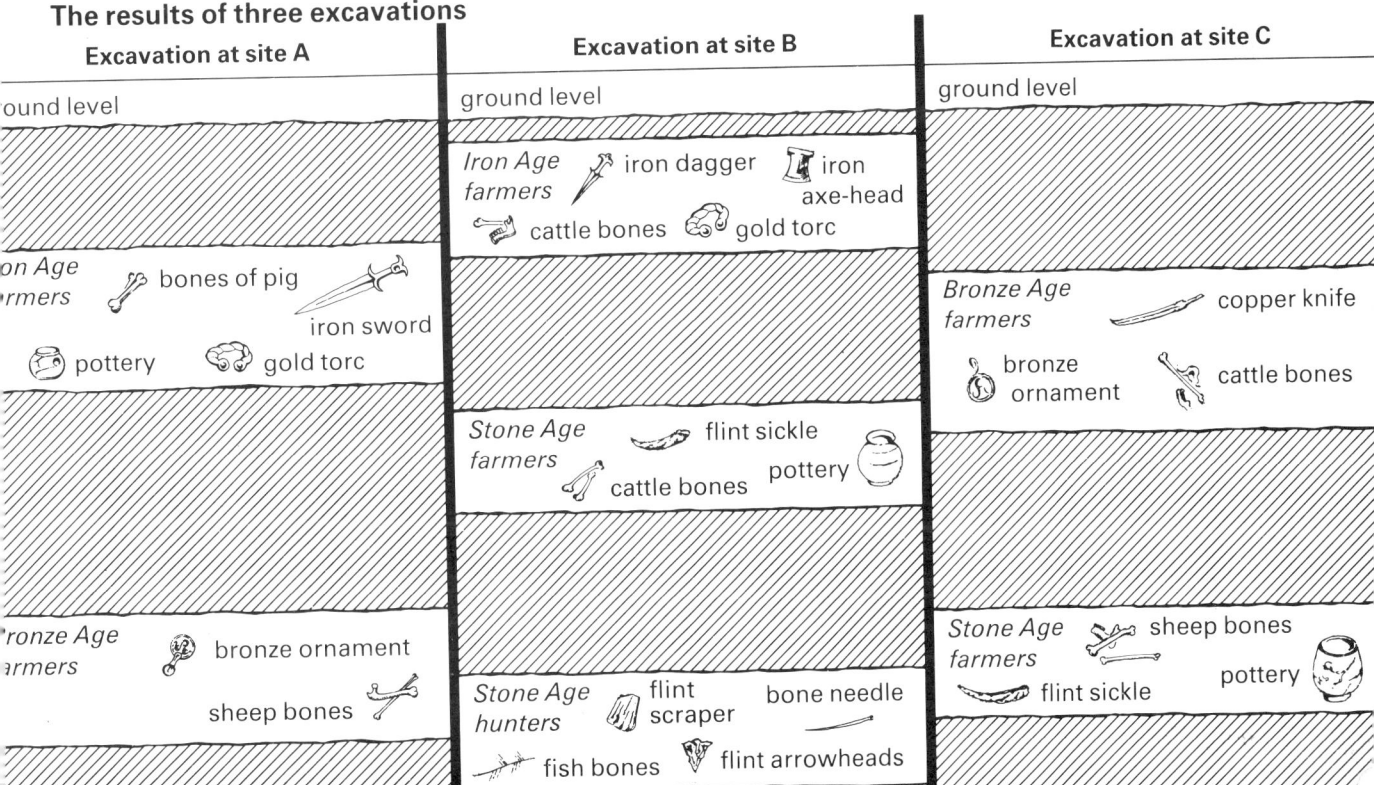

3. Prehistoric farmers

People who used stone

Look at the photograph below. It shows the entrance to the West Kennet Long Barrow in Wiltshire. This was the burial place for over 46 people who died about 4500 years ago. Their relatives built a number of burial chambers with stones like these. They covered them over with large stones resting on top (like those at Stonehenge). You can see the inside of this chamber on page 56. Earth was later piled over the stone burial chambers to make a long earth mound, called a long barrow.

• Use the height of the girl (about 1.6m tall) to help you guess the height of the four largest stones shown in the photograph. How wide are they?
• How many people do you think would have been needed to lift the biggest stone? How do you think these prehistoric people, who had no machines, could move large stone blocks into position like this?

A Neolithic flint dagger

The Neolithic period

The people who built the West Kennet Long Barrow are known as the Neolithic or New Stone Age farmers. They probably came to Britain from what is now France and Spain. These early farmers brought with them skills which the Stone Age hunters of Britain had not yet learned about. The New Stone Age farmers knew how to cultivate fields, sow seed and harvest grain. They reared cattle, sheep and pigs. We know this because bones from these animals have been found in New Stone Age camps like the one at Windmill Hill in Wiltshire (close to the West Kennet Long Barrow). Flint sickles tell us that they harvested corn.

They are called Neolithic (*Neo = New* and *Lith = Stone*) because their tools were made of stone, not metal. You can see a sharp flint Neolithic dagger in the photograph. They are called *New* to distinguish them from the Stone Age hunters who lived in the *Old* and *Middle* Stone Ages.

The Neolithic farmers brought many new skills with them besides farming. They made pottery to hold their grain and milk. They did this by moulding wet clay and baking it hard in a fire. They tanned animal skins to make leather for their clothes. As you can see on pages 51–52, they also sank deep pits to get the best flints for their tools.

A Neolithic farm

Silbury Hill

A Neolithic village

The picture above shows the type of village the Neolithic farmers probably built in southern England over 4000 years ago. We don't know exactly what they looked like, because little evidence of this has been discovered so far.

However, a Neolithic village built of stone was discovered by accident at Skara Brae in Scotland. It was revealed when storms uncovered some sand dunes on the coast of the Orkneys. The photograph on page 24 shows what the inside of one of the houses in this Neolithic village looked like. It is not hard to picture people using this room over 4000 years ago. There would be a fire in the hearth

in the centre of the room, food in the stone cupboard and heather or soft turf in the stone beds on either side of the room.

● Compare this photograph and the picture above with the picture of the Stone Age hunters on page 5. Make a list of the ways in which the everyday life of these Neolithic farmers was more advanced than that of the Stone Age hunters.

Silbury Hill

There are many other things we don't know about the Neolithic peoples. Why did they build the huge artificial hill at Silbury in Wiltshire? You can see it in the middle of the photograph, which was taken from the West Kennet Long Barrow. It is about 40m high and was built in about 2500 B.C. A team of 1000 men would have taken 5 to 10 years to build it! Archaeologists have excavated the site, but so far no-one can be sure why it was built.

●What do you think might have been the reason for the hill? How do you think the Neolithic people planned it? How do you think they organised its construction?

History skill : drawing a field sketch

Imagine you have gone on a school outing to Wiltshire and that your visit includes trips to Silbury Hill and West Kennet. Draw field sketches of the West Kennet Long Barrow and Silbury Hill. Sketches are simple drawings labelled with measurements (such as the height of the hill names of places, and notes on details to be seen such as colours, types of stone, etc.).

Bronze Age people

People who used bronze

Look at the photograph above showing Castlerigg Stone Circle in the English Lake District. Can you imagine the same scene over 3500 years ago when prehistoric people, like those shown in the picture on the right, could have been seen here?

- Draw a field sketch of this stone circle.
- Show on it a number of Bronze Age people at Castlerigg in about 1500 B.C.

The Bronze Age people are so called because they made many of their tools, implements and ornaments from bronze.

- Find out what metals are used to make bronze. Why is it a more useful material for making tools and implements than the flint used in the Stone Age? Has it any disadvantages compared with stone or flint? Is it as hard? Is it as easily found? Is it easy to shape tools and weapons from bronze?

Exactly why these Bronze Age people built stone circles like Castlerigg or Stonehenge is still a mystery. Some people think they may have been used as temples. Others think they may have been built in order to calculate

when midsummer day would fall. You can read more about this on pages 58–59.

Where prehistoric people lived in the British Isles

distribution of Neolithic monuments

×× distribution of beakers of the early Bronze Age

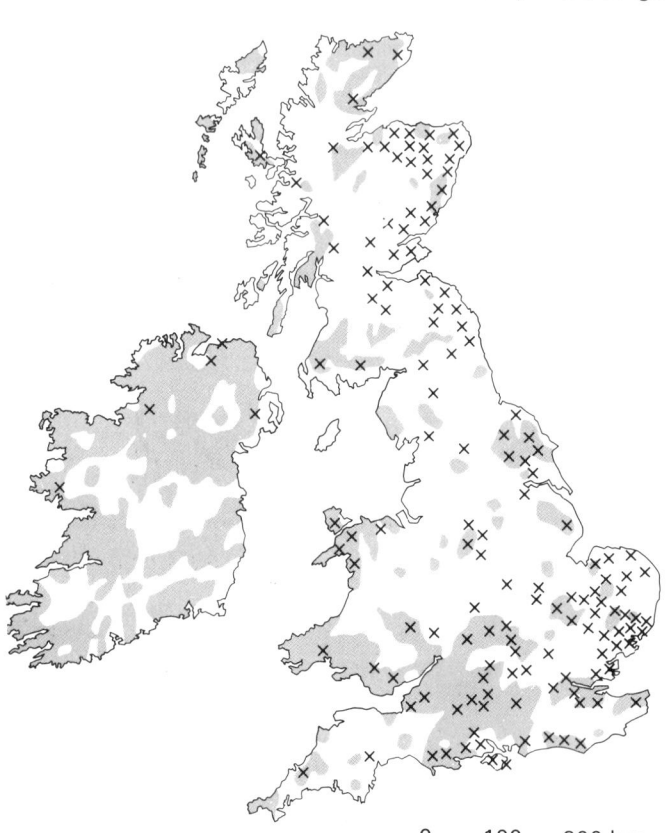

0   100   200 km

The Beaker people

The first Bronze Age people came to Britain about 4000 years ago. They are known as the Beaker people because of the shape of the pots they used for drinking. Some of these beakers have been found under burial mounds. You can see roughly where they lived in the map opposite. This marks the places where these Bronze Age beakers have been discovered. The map also shows where the Neolithic people built stone burial chambers and other monuments.

• Write one or two sentences to say in which parts of the British Isles most of the discoveries about the Beaker people have been made. Where are most of the Neolithic monuments situated?
• Which areas of the British Isles seem to have been settled by both groups of people?
• Find the position of your town or village on this map. Is your local museum likely to have many finds which tell us about (a) the Neolithic people (b) the Bronze Age people?

Use of flints in the Bronze Age

Some Stone Age hunters would have continued to live in parts of Britain long after the Neolithic farmers began to grow crops and rear cattle and sheep. Likewise, there was no sudden jump from the Stone Age into the Bronze Age. People continued to use flints and other stones for many tools long after they knew how to use copper and bronze.

Trade

One group of Bronze Age farmers lived on Salisbury Plain in Wiltshire and organized the building of Stonehenge. They are thought to have been led by powerful chiefs. It would have needed great leaders to control the building of such a massive monument.

They were also well organized in other ways. They traded goods with people living in other lands. We know this because some of the goods found on Bronze Age sites could only have come from areas a considerable distance away — such as gold from Ireland and tin from Cornwall.

History skill : using a map

We can learn something about life in prehistoric times by studying modern maps. The one below shows the district around Avebury in Wiltshire.

Make a tracing of this map. Show on it only the Neolithic sites — the camp at Windmill Hill, the long barrows, Silbury Hill and the Sanctuary (a Neolithic temple made of wood). What do you notice about the position of these Neolithic remains?

Make another tracing of this map but show on it only Avebury Stone Circle, the Stone Avenue and the Sanctuary. What do you notice about the position of these Neolithic and Bronze Age remains?

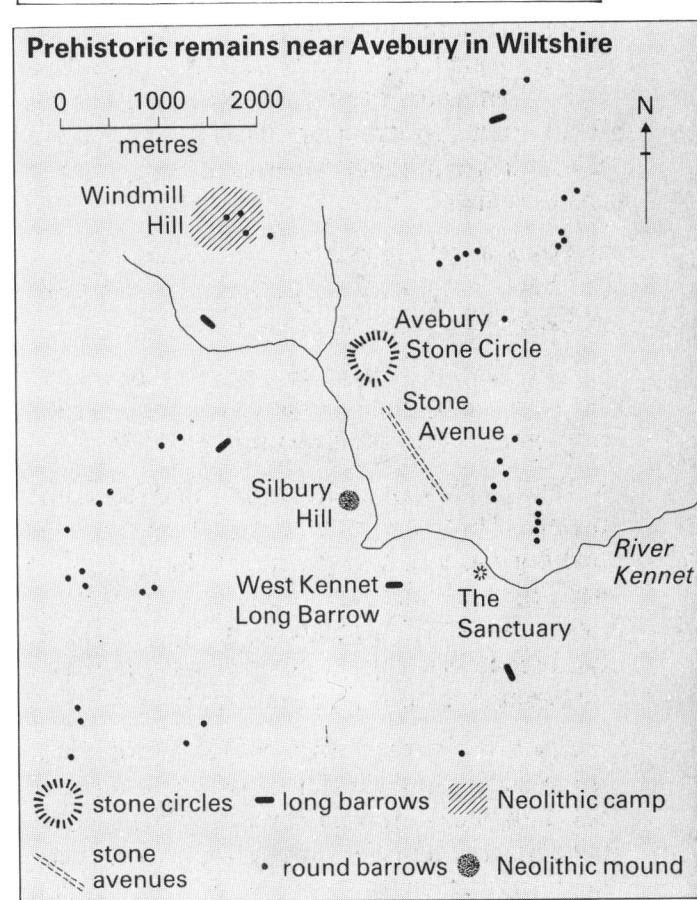

Prehistoric remains near Avebury in Wiltshire

The Iron Age man found at Tollund in Denmark

Warrior's helmet found in the Thames at Waterloo Bridge

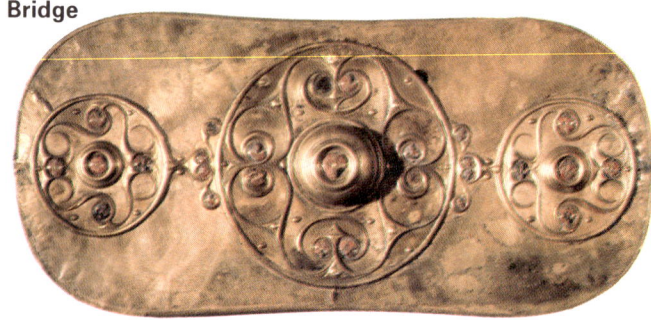

Bronze shield from the Iron Age — found in the Thames at Battersea

People who used iron

Look at this photograph. It shows the face of an Iron Age man who lived in Denmark about 2000 years ago. His body was found in 1950. It had been preserved in a peat bog. The features of the man are so clear you can see the stubble on his chin.

- What does this tell you about him?

Doctors who examined his body discovered the remains of plants and seeds in his stomach. They believe his last meal was a thick soup made from barley and from plants which we would nowadays call weeds.

Detailed information like this about the people who lived in prehistoric times is very rare indeed. Archaeologists call him the Tollund Man after the place where he was found. They believe he was killed — perhaps as a sacrifice — and then thrown in the bogland. There was a leather rope around his neck and he wore a pointed leather cap which fastened under his chin like a bonnet.

The Iron Age

The Iron Age is the name given to the period in prehistoric times when people first began to use iron. In Britain this was about 2800 years ago. In fact, many people in Britain continued to use bronze or flint for their tools and made little or no use of iron. Most of the people who used iron at this time lived in south-eastern England.

Iron was a very useful material for tools and weapons. It could be shaped as a hoop and used to cover the outer surface of a wooden wheel — as on a chariot or cart.

- Why was a chariot with iron-covered wheels better than one with wooden wheels?

Iron could also be used to make strong ploughs which could dig over fields of heavy clay. Ploughmen in the Bronze Age had been unable to cultivate heavy fields like these. Iron could also be used to make sharp axe-heads which could clear thick forests. Iron swords were far superior to those made of bronze.

The Iron Age warrior tribes

By this time the people of Rome had built a fine city. They were already conquering the lands which were to form their empire. When their soldiers and travellers returned to Rome, they described the native peoples they had seen in countries like Britain.

The great Roman leader Julius Caesar led two expeditions to England in 55 B.C. and 54 B.C. He described the fort defended by one of the British tribes as 'a place with an embankment and a ditch'. He also admired the skill of the British warriors and their charioteers. This is what he wrote.

'First they drive all over the battlefield hurling their spears, often throwing our troops into confusion with the sound of their horses and the clatter of their chariot wheels.'

The chariots had a crew of two : a driver and a warrior. The charioteers were brilliant horsemen who could keep the horses going at full gallop and then abruptly change direction or come to a sudden halt.

Another Roman writer said the Iron Age tribesmen put chalk into their hair to make it stand on end. Other writers said the Britons decorated their bodies with a blue warpaint called woad. All this was designed to put fear in the hearts of the enemy. During a battle the Druids (priests) blew long trumpets to urge the warriors to fight with bravery and skill.

Iron Age hill forts

All over southern England the Iron Age tribes built hilltop forts with deep ditches and embankments (or ramparts) made of earth. Spiked wooden fences on top of the ramparts enclosed a large compound where the huts of the tribesmen were built. One of the largest and most impressive of these hill forts was at Maiden Castle in Dorset, which you can see in the photograph.

> **History skill : using your imagination**
> Imagine you are a prehistoric television reporter! Use the information on these pages (including the pictures) to write a vivid description of the storming of an Iron Age hill fort by a hostile tribe. Make your account as exciting as possible. Use the descriptions by Roman writers as if they were eyewitnesses being interviewed for the programme.

Replica of an Iron Age chariot at Cockley Cley, Norfolk

The Iron Age hill fort at Maiden Castle, Dorset

4. The Romans

Plaque erected at Deal in Kent

Julius Caesar

Julius Caesar

The photograph above was taken on the sea front at Deal in Kent.

- Why was the tablet erected at Deal in 1946?
- Find Deal on an atlas map. How far is it from the coast of Europe? From which part of Europe do you think Julius Caesar sailed?

Julius Caesar was one of the greatest leaders the world has ever known. He was a good speaker, a writer and a politician. He was also a successful soldier and conquered Gaul (now France) for the Romans.

Rome

Rome itself was a large city near the coast in central Italy. You can see a view of Rome as it looked about 2000 years ago in the picture on the facing page.

- Write a sentence to describe one of the ways in which the people of Rome were far more advanced then the Iron Age tribes-people of Britain.

At its peak, Rome may have had as many as one million inhabitants. They lived in a huge city with many slums and many splendid public buildings. The ruins of some of these buildings, such as the Colosseum where wild beast shows were held, can still be seen today.

Rome became powerful and her armies began to conquer other lands around the Mediterranean, in North Africa and in Europe. During his campaigns in Gaul, Julius Caesar was annoyed by the help the Britons gave to their friends and allies in Gaul. So in 55 B.C. and 54 B.C. Julius Caesar led a force of soldiers and sailors to England. He forced the native British tribes to agree to his terms.

We can describe the events of these campaigns in some detail because, as you have already learned, Caesar wrote a description of his war in Gaul and against the Britons. The Romans were among the first people to leave written descriptions of life in Britain in the Iron Age. This is called written evidence.

Written evidence

As you can appreciate, describing events is very different from the evidence provided by archaeological discoveries. Excavations enable us to see the actual relics, remains and ruins of the past. They don't tell us what people thought, what they did and why they did it.

Written accounts help to give a more vivid impression of life in the past. The disadvantage is that they are not always strictly accurate. The writers may not always have been truthful. Sometimes they copied tales and stories from untrustworthy people.

Look at these descriptions of Britain:

1. 'Much of the island is level and thickly wooded although there are also many hills. It produces corn, cattle, gold, silver, iron, skins, slaves and hunting dogs. The people live in forts in the forests. They clear trees and erect a circular fence of stakes and build their huts and cattle pens within.' (Strabo)

2. 'The inhabitants of England live in poor cottages covered with thatch or branches. When they cut their corn they cut the ears off from the stalk and keep them in underground pits.' (Diodorus)

3. 'There are many farms and many cattle. They use gold coins and sometimes bars of iron. All the Britons cover themselves with blue woad.' (Julius Caesar)

4. 'They thresh their corn inside a large barn because the weather is dull and wet; they make bread and brew beer from corn, and mead from honey. In the north there is less farming since the weather is colder.' (Pytheas)

History skill : looking at evidence

Read the extracts through carefully. Make a list of the facts which tell us about farming in Britain 2000 years ago. Which of the facts quoted by the writers might be difficult to prove 2000 years later? Why can't we be absolutely certain life in Britain was like this then? How can eyewitnesses sometimes be mistaken?

Rome

The Roman conquest

Look at this tombstone to a soldier, Flavinus. He was killed at the age of 25, fighting in the Roman army against the Britons.

● Write two or three sentences describing Flavinus from this photograph. What weapon was he armed with? Was he an infantryman or a cavalryman? He is shown carrying a long pole with some sort of emblem at the top. Look at the pictures at the foot of these pages and write down the name of the type of soldier you think he was.

● A man is shown lying on the ground under the hooves of the horse. How can you tell he was supposed to be a defeated British tribesman? (Clue : Turn the picture sideways and examine the tribesman's hair.)

● Use the facts you have discovered so far to write a brief description of the Roman soldier Flavinus.

A stone carving like this is another piece of evidence which can be used to tell us about life in the past.

The Roman conquest of Britain came nearly one hundred years after the expeditions of Julius Caesar. In A.D. 43 a Roman army landed at Richborough in Kent and soon established its headquarters at Colchester in south-eastern England. One legion commanded by Vespasian, a future Emperor of Rome, defeated the British tribesmen at Maiden Castle hill fort. The Romans used ballistae — a type of mechanical catapult — to fire metal arrows at the Maiden Castle warriors. They were armed mainly with slings and large pebbles which they hurled at the Romans.

We know about this battle because the remains of the defeated Britons have been discovered in a 'war cemetery' just outside the eastern entrance to the hill fort.

● Look at the photograph showing the replica of a ballista which can be seen on display on the site of the Roman fort of Vindolanda in Northumberland. Write a sentence to say how you think this machine could be used to fire a metal bolt.

centurion

praetorian guard battle

tribune

hastatus

Hadrian's Wall

Other Roman legions slowly conquered western and northern England. The Picts in Scotland were a difficult tribe to conquer. Eventually, in A.D. 122, the Romans began to build a wall separating England from Scotland. It is called Hadrian's Wall after the Emperor who ordered it to be built. You will find out more about the Wall on page 30.

The Roman army was an extremely efficient fighting force. Its crack troops were Roman citizens — the legionaries. Each legion of about 5500 men was divided into 10 cohorts and was led by 60 centurions, six tribunes and a commanding officer.

History skill : using an atlas
Look at an atlas map of England and find the county of Northumberland. Use the atlas map to help you draw a map of Hadrian's Wall. Draw an outline of the coastline of southern Scotland and northern England. Mark in the course of the Wall. Use a dot to show the position of the town of Wallsend and the position of any forts along the length of the Wall which are shown on the map, such as Housesteads, Chesters and Vindolanda. What does the position of the town of Wallsend tell you about Hadrian's Wall?

Roman Britons

Many Britons welcomed the Romans. Some became very wealthy landowners and built splendid villas, like the palatial mansion believed to have been built for King Cogidubnus at Fishbourne in Sussex. He was the leader of a British tribe called the Atrebates. His palace, which was built about 1900 years ago, had many magnificent rooms with mosaic floors and marble walls. Other Britons were less fortunate, and some fought bitterly against the Romans.

legionary

veles

praetorian guard dress

19

Statue of Queen Boudicca at Westminster bridge, London

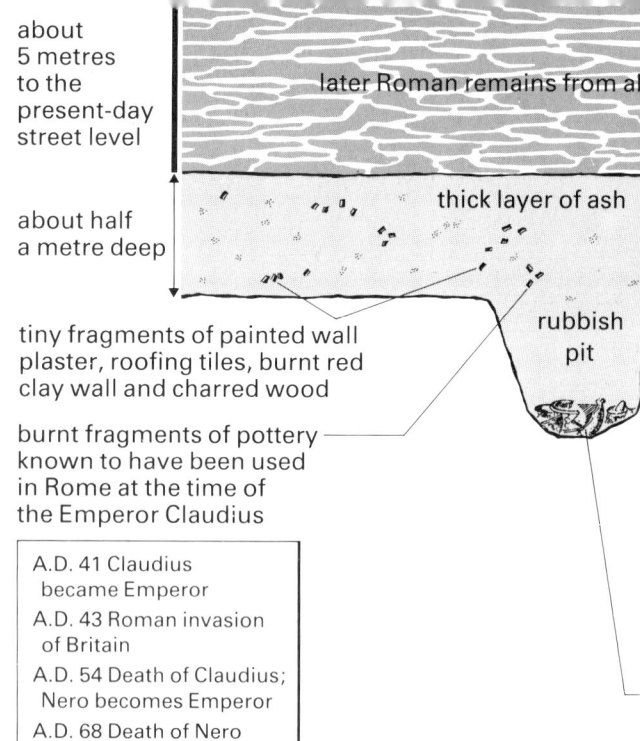

about 5 metres to the present-day street level

later Roman remains from ab

thick layer of ash

about half a metre deep

tiny fragments of painted wall plaster, roofing tiles, burnt red clay wall and charred wood

rubbish pit

burnt fragments of pottery known to have been used in Rome at the time of the Emperor Claudius

A.D. 41 Claudius became Emperor
A.D. 43 Roman invasion of Britain
A.D. 54 Death of Claudius; Nero becomes Emperor
A.D. 68 Death of Nero

Results of many excavations in London (similar finds have been made at Colchester and St Albans)

Boudicca's revolt

Queen Boudicca (sometimes known as Boadicea) was the leader of the Iceni tribe in East Anglia. When her husband died she was mistreated by the Romans. So she and her tribesmen destroyed the newly-built Roman towns of Colchester, St Albans and London and set them on fire.

We know about this from two of the different types of evidence which help historians to find out what happened in the past. Look at this evidence carefully.

1. A written description by the Roman writer Tacitus who wrote this account in about A.D. 100.

'During the consulship of Caesonius Paetus and Petronius Turpilianus, a dreadful disaster happened to the army in Britain. While the Britons were preparing to revolt, the statue of victory at Colchester fell down as if surrendering to the enemy. Colchester had only a handful of soldiers to defend it. The Temple there was strongly fortified so this was where the army hoped to make its last stand. But few other precautions were taken. They didn't dig a ditch or build a spiked fence; nor were the women and the elderly sent out of the town. They were completely unprepared, and so badly guarded that when the attack came, they were taken by surprise and overwhelmed by the Barbarians. The town was laid waste with fire and sword. Only the Temple held out, but after a siege of two days, was taken by storm.

Of those who remained behind in London not one escaped the anger of the Barbarians. The inhabitants of Verulamium (St Albans) were likewise put to the sword.'

(Caesonius Paetus and Petronius Turpilianus were consuls in Rome in A.D. 61.)

2. Archaeological discoveries in London, Colchester and St Albans seem to confirm the account written by Tacitus. Those finds which have been made in London are shown in the diagram above, even though they were actually discovered in many different places over a long period of time.

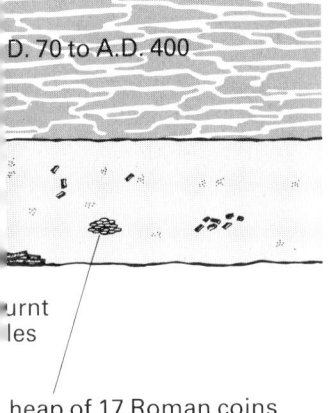

urnt
les

heap of 17 Roman coins
- badly burnt and some
artly melted and joined
o one another; 15 of these
oins were minted at the
me of the Emperor Claudius

ieces of broken pottery
iade at the time of
laudius and Nero

Roman fort at Richborough, Kent

History skill : detective work among the ruins

Look at the diagram showing the results of the excavations in London. Use the clues in the picture and in the account by Tacitus to answer these questions.

1. How do we know it was a great fire?
2. How do we know many houses were burnt down? Write a sentence to say what these houses were built of.
3. How do we know the fire took place after the Roman invasion in A.D. 43?
4. How do we know the fire probably took place at some time during the reign of the Emperor Nero (A.D. 54 to 68)? Give reasons why it was unlikely to have occurred much before A.D. 54 or later than A.D. 68.
5. Many experts believe Boudicca's revolt took place in A.D. 60. When did Tacitus say it took place?
6. In what ways was Colchester unprepared for an attack? What preparations should have been made?
7. What did the Romans call the Iceni?
8. What worried people who were superstitious in Colchester before the attack?
9. Write a paragraph to describe the destruction of Colchester, London and St Albans using only information which you can get from studying Tacitus and the results of the excavations.

Boudicca's revolt was quickly put down by other Roman soldiers. New towns were built over the ruins of Colchester, London and St Albans. Many other new towns were built throughout Britain.

For two or three hundred years, the people of southern Britain lived in peace under Roman rule. But attacks by Saxon pirates became serious in the third century, so the Romans built a series of coastal forts, like the one at Richborough in Kent, which you can see in the photograph.

The Saxon attacks became stronger in the fourth century. By this time other 'barbarians' were attacking many other parts of the Roman Empire as well. So in A.D. 410 the Romans finally abandoned their British colony, leaving it to the mercy of the Saxons in Denmark and Germany and the Picts in Scotland.

21

5. Prehistoric homes

History skill : making a time-chart
Complete the time-chart you started on page 5 and add an entry for the Middle Stone Age people shown in this picture.

A Mesolithic (Middle Stone Age) settlement

The picture shows an artist's drawing of a Middle Stone Age (or Mesolithic) settlement. This was the period which came before the New Stone Age (or Neolithic period) when people first learned to farm. These fishermen and hunters of about 10 000 years ago were much more advanced in their way of life than the cave people of the Old Stone Age you can read about on pages 4–5.

Excavations at a site near Scarborough in Yorkshire have proved that Middle Stone Age people built a settlement there by the side of what was once a lake. They used tree trunks, branches and earth to make a brushwood platform over part of the marsh. We can't be certain what their homes actually looked like, since these were probably only simple shelters. The homes were also made from branches and earth.

● Why did the Middle Stone Age people build a brushwood platform? Why do you think archaeologists are unable to say what the homes of these people looked like?

The Middle Stone Age people lived by hunting wild animals such as red deer, elk, wild pig and wild oxen. They also caught fish. Archaeologists have discovered an object which they believe may have been a wooden paddle. They think the fishermen may have used hollowed-out tree trunks for boats. Their weapons included barbed harpoons made from deer antlers to spear the fish. They also used wooden spears, and bows and arrows tipped with sharp flint arrowheads. Some Middle Stone Age hunters trained hunting dogs to help them chase wild animals. Some used fishing nets and fishing lines with barbed hooks. Their tools included flint axes and flint scrapers (to remove flesh from animal skins). They also used flint knives or chisels for carving wood, bone and antler.

Study of Stone Age people, who live today in remote parts of the world, has led experts to think that the job of collecting wild fruits, nuts, seeds and berries for food was probably left to the women and children. But we can't be sure of this. Nor can we be sure that it was the women who made clothes by sewing the skins of animals with bone needles.

● Why not? Why isn't it possible to prove this?

A Neolithic hut

The photograph below shows the living room of a Stone Age house built about 4500 years ago. It is one of a small group of seven huts at the prehistoric village of Skara Brae.

● Draw a sketch of this Neolithic living room and label these features, (a) the hearth where a fire burned in the middle of the hut, (b) two beds marked out by stone slabs at the sides of the hut, (c) a stone cupboard where food was probably kept.

Each stone hut in this village has a main room like this, about 4 to 6 metres square. Earth or clay covered the flagstones on the outside walls of each hut. The roofs were probably made from animal skins or sods of earth laid across pieces of driftwood or whalebone. There were few trees in this bleak part of Scotland, so the New Stone Age people who lived here had to use stone as their main building material.

Neolithic hut at Skara Brae, Orkney

● How do you think these Neolithic people made their stone beds comfortable places in which to sleep? What could they use for blankets and pillows?

History skill : finding out from archaeological discoveries

Look at this list of some of the archaeological discoveries which have been made in the huts at Skara Brae. Write down two or three sentences to say what types of people you think lived here in the New Stone Age. What food do you think they ate? What else do these discoveries tell you about life at Skara Brae 4500 years ago?

large number of empty shells	peat ash
bone pins	stone cups
bead necklaces	deer bones
stone chisels	sheep bones
stone axeheads	cattle bones
axe handles made from driftwood	clay pottery

How do we know they were Neolithic peoples?

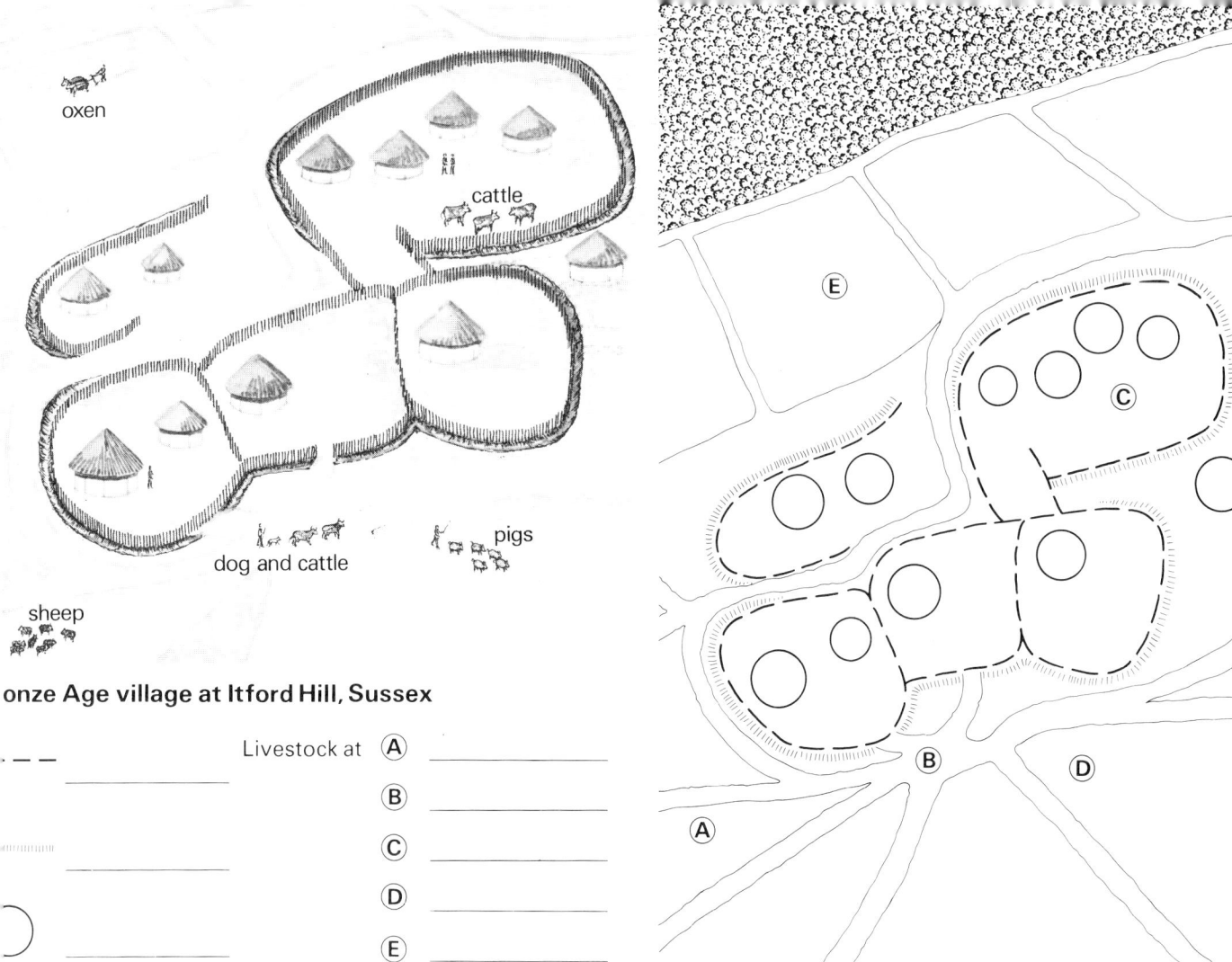

oxen

cattle

dog and cattle

pigs

sheep

onze Age village at Itford Hill, Sussex

	Livestock at	(A)	
		(B)	
		(C)	
		(D)	
		(E)	

A Bronze Age village

This is the sort of view you might have seen had you been able to fly over a village on the chalk downs of Sussex about 3000 years ago. As you can see, there are a number of huts and they are surrounded by small fields. The people who lived here at Itford Hill were Bronze Age farmers.

● How many huts are shown here?
● Write a description of one of these huts, saying what it is made of and describing its shape. How do you think the thatched roof stayed in position? What stopped it from falling down? What building materials did they use? Why did they build the houses with thatched roofs?
● Why do you think these Bronze Age farmers dug a ditch and built a spiked wooden fence all the way round the village?
● What shape are the fields? What are they used for?

History skill : using a map
Look at the outline map and compare it with the aerial view of the Bronze Age village. Make a copy of this map. Name the livestock you would expect to see at points A,B,C,D,E on the plan. Write on your copy of the map the meaning of each of the symbols shown at the bottom of the map.

An Iron Age village

The picture on this page shows an Iron Age village in about 100 B.C.. This was over a thousand years after the village shown on page 25.

● Write a detailed description of this Iron Age village. Say how it differs from a modern village. Is it very different from the Bronze Age village on page 25?

The Iron Age tribes often built their villages inside the ramparts of a hill fort. Some of their houses may have been common huts for use by all the members of the tribe. Remains of eleven round huts from the Iron Age were discovered when Heathrow Airport was being built near London.

We know about the types of houses these tribespeople built because archaeologists have found post holes which show where they stood. Almost all of these houses had sloping roofs which allowed rain to drain away easily. The easiest type of sloping roof to construct was one where timber posts held up the rafters on the roof. These posts were driven into holes in the ground, so that they wouldn't fall over easily. When the huts were abandoned or caught fire, the remains of the thatched roof decayed and the walls of earth crumbled to dust. But where the wooden posts were sunk into the ground, the wood rotted away and left stains and traces. A trained archaeologist can identify these today as the old post holes. So if the post holes are in the shape of a circle, we can picture a round hut. If they are in the shape of a rectangle, we can picture a long building. Sometimes the post holes were made in solid rock, such as chalk, which is quite easy to scoop out.

• The Iron Age village shown in the picture is based on information about the real village which once stood on the site of Heathrow Airport. Draw a rough plan to show the type of pattern you think the archaeologists may have seen when they discovered the foundations for these buildings.

• One of these wooden buildings is thought to have been a temple, because it is similar in appearance to the stone temples which were built in ancient Greece. Label your plan to show the position of the temple.

Chysauster Iron Age village

Visitors to the Iron Age village at Chysauster in Cornwall (seen in the photographs below) can see stone huts which were built in about 100 B.C. They were occupied during much of the time the Romans lived in Britain.

The village consisted of nine houses built along a village street. Excavations have shown that each of these houses had its own plot of land. It was roughly circular in shape and surrounded by stone walls like those you can see in the photograph. Each house had a central courtyard or compound where the animals could be kept safe at night. One or two small huts were built along the edge of the compound for use as farm buildings, workshops or storerooms. The thatched hut where the family lived had a hearth for a fire. In some huts you can still see the grinding stone which was used to make flour from grain. Some buildings had underground drains as well.

> **History skill : looking at a clue**
> One of the interesting things you can see at the Chysauster Iron Age village today is shown in the bottom right-hand photograph. This stone stood in the middle of a house where an Iron Age family lived about 2000 years ago. The walls of their house were made of stone but the roof probably consisted of branches covered over with turf or thatch.
>
> What do you think this stone was used for?

Iron Age house at Chysauster, Cornwall

Stone found in one of the huts at Chysauster, Cornwall

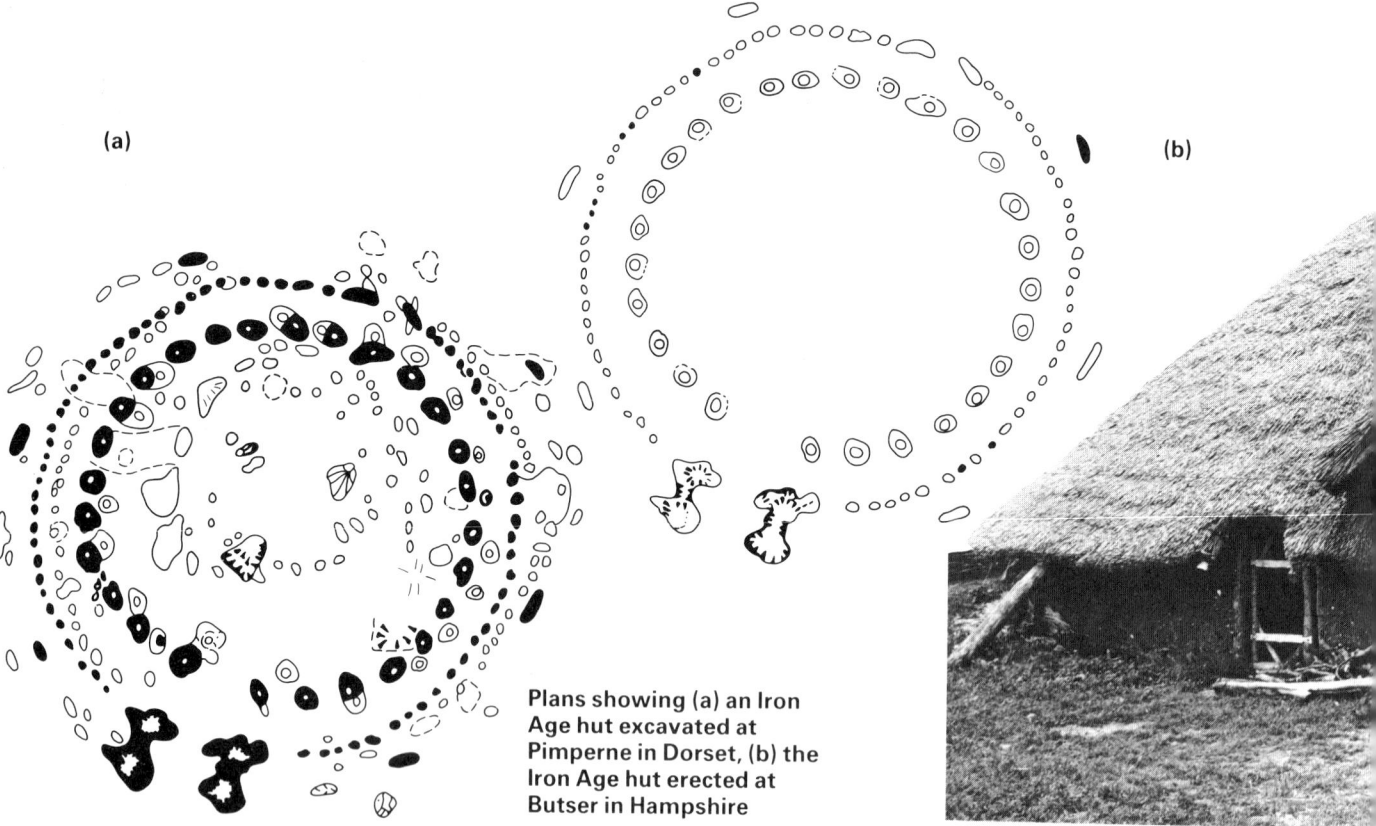

(a)

(b)

Plans showing (a) an Iron Age hut excavated at Pimperne in Dorset, (b) the Iron Age hut erected at Butser in Hampshire

Butser Iron Age farm

Look at these plans showing how the Iron Age house, seen in the photograph above, was built. The plan on the left shows the post holes which were uncovered at a place called Pimperne in Dorset. They had been carved into white chalk.

This plan of a real Iron Age hut was simplified by the people who built the Iron Age hut at Butser in Hampshire which visitors can see today. This is not a genuine Iron Age hut, but it has been built skilfully with Iron Age tools. A visitor today has the exciting experience of being able to enter the type of hut which was used by our prehistoric ancestors. The plan on the right shows the one which was used when this hut was erected.

● How many entrances are there to this hut?
● Why are two circles of post holes shown on the plan? Which circle do you think shows the posts which held up the roof? What do you think the other circle of posts was used for?

● Write a description of this Iron Age hut in such detail that someone who has not seen it can still picture it clearly.

Building the hut
When the Iron Age hut at Butser was built, the people involved had to fell over 200 trees to provide the posts and rafters for the roof. Over ten tonnes of mud had to be mixed with clay, straw and hair to make the material which was used for the walls. This was plastered or daubed on to a wooden framework. It is called *daub*, and this method of building walls was widely used in the Middle Ages as well. Four tonnes of straw were also needed for the steeply sloping roof. You can imagine the weight of this. The posts holding it up had to be strong and firmly planted in the ground.

● Make a drawing of the Butser Iron Age hut by tracing over the outline shown in the photograph. Then pencil in where you think the posts were which held up the roof and the rafters which stopped the straw from falling

Everyday objects used in the Iron Age:

tankard
mirror
safety pin
fire-dog
helmet
bucket
torc
shield

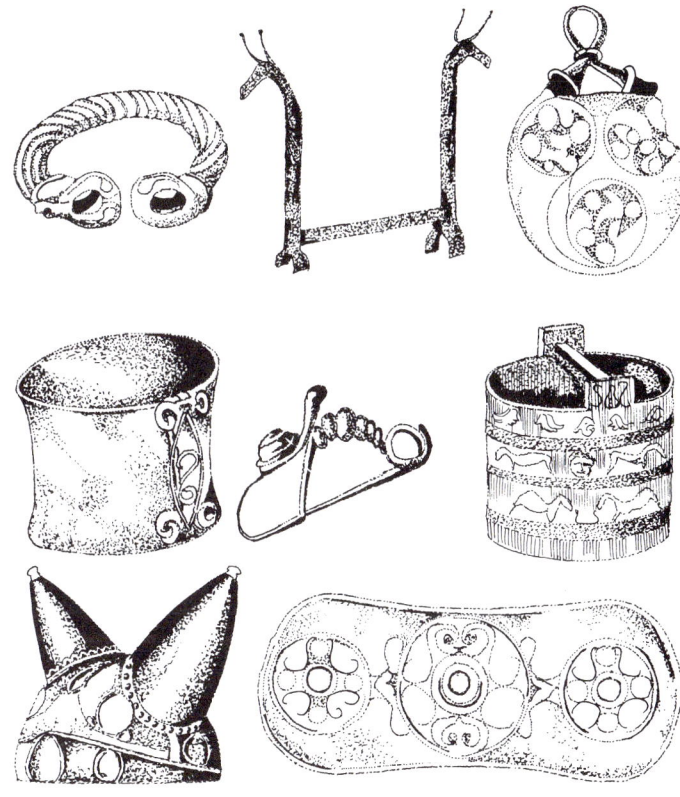

The reconstructed Iron Age hut at Butser

through. Label the parts of the building made from daub.

Although the hut looks quite small compared with a modern house, it is really very big. The floor of the hut is about 13 metres in diameter and the roof top is about 11 metres off the ground. It is said that 'many a modern house would fit inside'!

The hut was completed by being fitted out with a clay oven in the centre of the room. This uses wood, but there is no hole in the roof to let the smoke out. This is because the experts building the hut felt that if it was open to the sky the draught might fan the flames too much. They have since discovered that the smoke can be used to cure bacon and it helps to keep the thatch free of insects and other pests.

Other Iron Age features in the hut include a loom which is like those the Iron Age people used to weave cloth (see page 53) and a round boat covered with skins, called a coracle.

History skill : studying in a museum

The Iron Age farm at Butser is one of Britain's newest and most original museums. Other museums too have reconstructed prehistoric huts like this, such as the one at Cockley Cley in Norfolk, which shows an Iron Age village of the Iceni tribe at the time of Queen Boudicca.

Many Iron Age tools, implements and ornaments can be seen in ordinary museums as well. The pictures above show just a few of the things which might have been seen in an Iron Age home over 2000 years ago. See if you can identify the objects shown. Try to find out what these objects were used for. Some are fairly obvious, since they look like similar modern objects. Others are more difficult, because we don't use objects like these any more.

If you visit a museum in your home area, make simple drawings of some of the interesting objects on display. Look at those which tell you about the prehistoric period you are most interested in — such as the Iron Age or the Old Stone Age.

6. Roman homes

A Roman fort

Look at this photograph taken from the air above Hadrian's Wall. It shows the remains of what used to be the home of about 1000 Roman soldiers over 1800 years ago.

- Write a sentence to describe the shape of this fort when seen from the air. What shape are the corners of the four walls?
- The fort was built on the south side of Hadrian's Wall which runs east to west

The North Gate at Housesteads

The Roman fort at Housesteads from the air

across northern England. Identify Hadrian's Wall in the photograph. In which direction was the camera pointing when the photograph was taken?

- The fort had four gates: East Gate, South Gate, West Gate, North Gate. Which of these gates is shown in the middle of the wall closest to the camera?
- The remains of the North Gate at Housesteads are shown in the photograph on the right. Make a tracing or copy of the aerial photograph. On your tracing use the letter N to mark in the position of the North Gate.
- The picture on the opposite page gives you a view of the fort at Housesteads as it might have looked from the air in about A.D. 150.

(a) What are barracks? Who lived there? In which parts of the fort were they situated?

(b) What is a granary? What is stored there? Why was it needed by the soldiers manning the fort?

(c) What do the letters C.O. stand for? Where was the C.O.'s villa situated?

(d) What was the name of the building from which the Roman commander could organize the day-to-day running of the fort? Where was this building situated? On your tracing, use an abbreviation to mark in the position of this building.

(e) What defences did the fort have?

The latrine building at Housesteads

important. At the Roman fort of Chesters, near Housesteads, you can see the remains of two bath-houses. One was for the use of the commander of the fort and the other for the use of his men.

Most Roman forts had an excellent source of water supply. The remains of wells and of special pipes or channels (called aqueducts), which brought fresh water from nearby streams, can be seen today.

● What other services were provided for the benefit of the soldiers who lived at Housesteads?

Sanitation and water supply

The Roman army was very efficient. Roman soldiers trained hard and lived a tough life. But they expected certain comforts when stationed abroad. Their standard of living was very much higher than that of the native Britons or the Picts in Scotland. At Housesteads they had the use of the latrine block which you can see in the photograph above.

● Find the location of the latrines on the aerial photograph and on the picture opposite. On your tracing use the letter L to mark the position of the latrines.

In Roman times this was the public lavatory for the camp. Seats were placed above the drains which you can see on either side of this room. They were regularly flushed with water. Fresh water also ran along the channels which you can see in the middle of the room. The soldiers used this water to rinse out the sponges attached to sticks, which the Romans used instead of toilet paper.

● What do you think was the purpose of the two stone bowls shown in the photograph?

As you can see, the Romans thought cleanliness and good sanitation were very

---

History skill : making a model
Make a model of the fort at Housesteads from modelling clay, using the aerial photograph and the picture to guide you. Use small paper flags on pins to indicate the position of all the important buildings. If this is not possible, then draw a map of the fort and write the names of the buildings as neatly as you can.

The fort at Housesteads as it might have looked about 1800 years ago

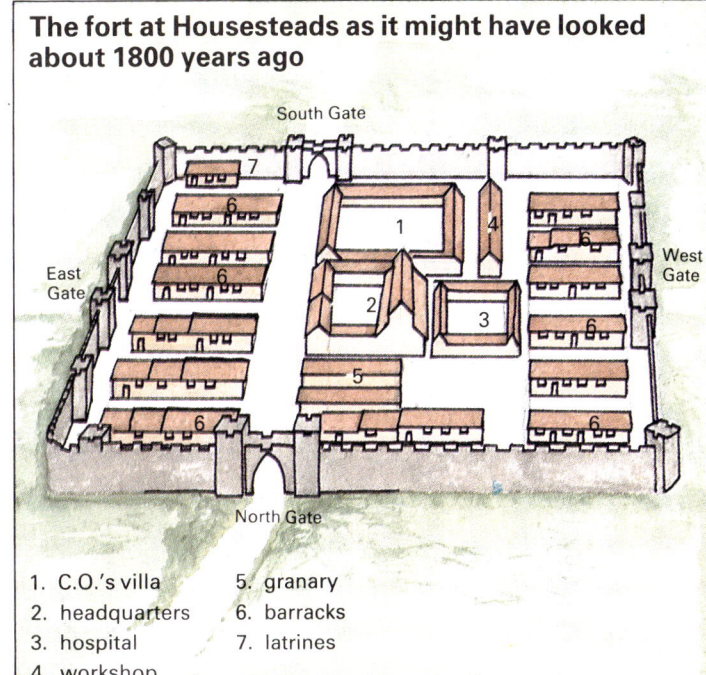

1. C.O.'s villa
2. headquarters
3. hospital
4. workshop
5. granary
6. barracks
7. latrines

A Roman villa

The photograph above shows a mosaic pavement which was discovered only recently at Fishbourne in Sussex.

● How do you think the mosaic pavement was laid? Write two or three sentences to say how you would set about constructing a similar mosaic today.

When archaeologists discover fragments of

a mosaic like this, they may begin to suspect they have found the remains of a Roman house or possibly a bath-house. Mosaic floors were expensive to lay, since they consisted of thousands of tiny pieces of coloured stone or sometimes glass. Floors like this would have been found only in the best rooms in a villa (a large country home), a big town house, or sometimes in a public bath-house.

Many of the villas in Britain were owned by Roman Britons who welcomed the Roman way of life. The most luxurious of these villas, at Fishbourne, is thought to have been owned by the leader of the Atrebates, a tribe who lived in what is now Hampshire and Sussex. Fishbourne had a large number of rooms with mosaic floors and some walls made of marble. Other villas were much smaller than this and were really no more than large farmhouses.

As you can see from the drawing below, a villa in Britain usually consisted of a squarish courtyard surrounded on two or three sides by farm buildings and the private residence of the owner.

● Write a short description of a villa and compare it with a large house you have seen in your home area — such as a house which has been made into a number of flats.

Pliny's villa

We can guess what it was like to live in a villa in Britain by reading what Roman writers had to say about their homes. A man called Pliny sent a letter to his friend Gallus which began 'You seem surprised I like my seaside villa at Laurentum so much'. He then went on to describe it in such detail that we can picture it today some 1900 years later.

'The villa is big enough for my needs and not too expensive to look after. There is a plain entrance hall, an inner courtyard and a splendid dining room with superb views of the sea. On one side of this room are the main living rooms, a library, a bedroom with warm air heating under the floor, and the rooms where my slaves and servants live. On the other side

The Roman villa at Rockbourne in Hampshire

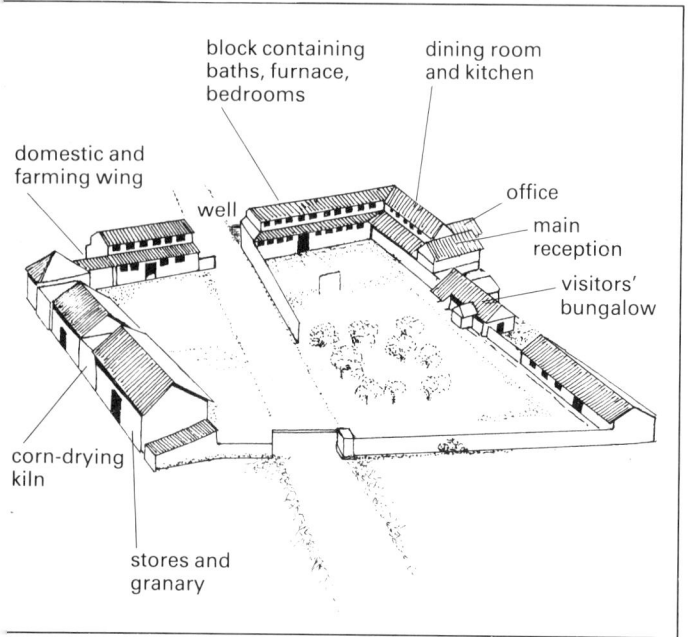

domestic and farming wing

block containing baths, furnace, bedrooms

dining room and kitchen

well

office

main reception

visitors' bungalow

corn-drying kiln

stores and granary

are several bedrooms and then the bath-house with its bath tubs, cold room and steam room. Close by is the heated pool where you can swim and a sunny courtyard for ball games.'

Other parts of his villa included several extra dining rooms, living rooms, bedrooms and storerooms for wine and grain. His garden was planted with box trees, rosemary, fig trees, violets and mulberry bushes. There was also his favourite summer house, where he could rest and sleep away from the noise in the house itself.

● Which was the most important room in Pliny's house?
● Warm air central heating under the floors was a marvellous Roman invention. Is it still to be found today? Why was it especially useful in the villas built in Britain?
● Did Pliny think his villa was large? Who looked after the house for him?

Rooms in a museum
You can imagine what it was like to live in a luxurious Roman house or villa if you go to a museum where rooms have been furnished to show what they might have looked like in Roman times. Two rooms in the Museum of London are shown in the photographs here.

● What were they used for? Draw pictures to show how you think rooms like these might have looked when in use in Roman Britain. How do they differ from similar rooms today?

The homes of ordinary people were far less luxurious. Thousands lived in the crowded slums of Rome itself. British towns were more spacious than this, but most people lived in small wooden homes rather than in villas or stone houses. In the countryside, Britons continued to live in huts like those you saw on pages 26–28.

● Write a sentence to say why we know much more about villas than about the homes of the poor.

Roman kitchen in the Museum of London

History skill : a written description
The drawing opposite shows a villa which has been excavated at Rockbourne in Hampshire. Imagine you are Pliny and you have left your villa at Laurentum to come and live here in England. Write a letter to Gallus, vividly describing your British villa. Use the other information and pictures on these pages to help you make your account as detailed as possible.

Roman living room in the Museum of London

33

7. Towns and town life

A Roman town

The first large settlements in Britain were probably the groups of huts which were built behind the ramparts of an Iron Age hill fort like Maiden Castle (see page 15). Although some had a temple and a market-place, we would nowadays call them villages rather than towns, since the buildings there were thatched farm huts made of wood. They were not permanent buildings of stone or brick like those which were built by the Romans.

● Why do you think the Romans who came to Britain immediately began to build towns?

The Roman towns in Britain were very like Rome itself (see picture on page 17). The forum or market-place stood in the town centre with the town hall (or basilica) on one side. Other buildings in the forum included temples, other public meeting places and long rows of shops. These often stood behind a row of columns, like an arcade or covered shopping precinct today. Unlike parts of Rome, however, Britain's towns were spacious and well-designed. They had wide streets, good drains, a piped water supply, public bath-houses and sometimes public lavatories. Rome had many narrow streets, crowded slums and drains which only served parts of the city. Only the well-to-do had a piped water supply. Not surprisingly, Rome was frequently ravaged with disease.

Much of what we know about Roman towns comes from studying Pompeii and Herculaneum. These Italian towns were covered by volcanic ash and mud when Vesuvius erupted in A.D. 79. Whole streets and buildings were preserved in this way, so that today we know how people lived and worked in a town about 1900 years ago. This information helps to explain features discovered on the sites of Roman towns in Britain.

History skill : finding out from clues

These are some of the things a visitor can
see in the streets of Pompeii today:
— deep ruts in the stones in the middle of
   one of the streets;
— long straight streets at right angles to
   each other;
— large stepping stones across a street;
— raised pavements on either side of the
   cobbled streets;
— channels in the streets below the kerbs
   of the pavements;
What do these observations tell you about
the streets of Pompeii in A.D. 79? Think
about what happened when it rained and
what the streets were like when carts
rumbled through, carrying heavy goods.

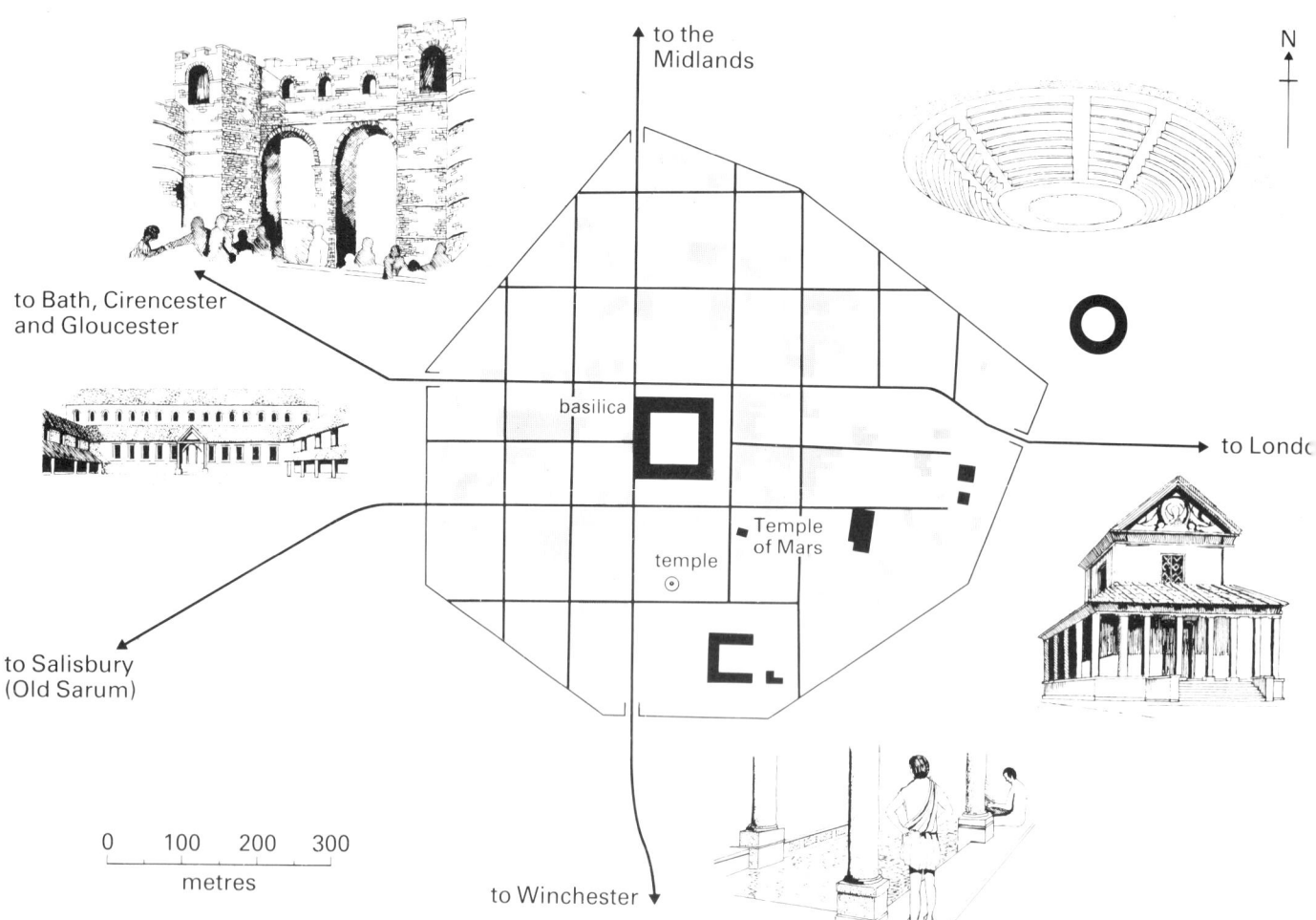

to the Midlands

N

to Bath, Cirencester and Gloucester

basilica

to London

Temple of Mars

temple

to Salisbury (Old Sarum)

0   100   200   300
metres

to Winchester

Silchester

Plan of Silchester. Right: Aerial photograph of Silchester

The map on this page shows the Roman town of Silchester in Hampshire. This is one of the few Roman towns to have disappeared completely. Other Roman towns like York, St Albans and London have grown into important cities today, but Silchester is now farmland. We know it was once a Roman city from the excavations which have been made there and from aerial photographs which show clearly the shape of the Roman city.

● How many walls did Silchester have? Write a sentence to describe the shape of the city. What coin-shape does it nearly resemble?

● Look at the map carefully and at the pictures in the margins which provide additional clues. Trace or copy the map and then name the following features:

(**a**) the North Gate, South Gate and East Gate

(**b**) the forum

(**c**) the amphitheatre

(**d**) the inn which lay to the south of the Temple of Mars

(**e**) the temples near the East Gate

(**f**) the public bath-house to the east of the Temple of Mars

(**g**) the West Gate which you would pass through if you came into Silchester from Cirencester

● How far would a Roman Briton have had to walk from the North Gate to the South Gate? How far was it from the West Gate to the East Gate? Is your town or village as big as this?

- Which building was outside the town walls? Where is a similar building to this to be found in your nearest town? Is it in the centre of that town or on the outskirts?
- Which buildings were in the centre of Silchester? What similar buildings are to be found in the centre of your nearest town?
- How would you try to convince a friend that the Romans planned Silchester as a new city right from the start?
- Name four ways in which Silchester resembled ancient Rome (see p. 17).

(see p. 17)

History skill : looking at an aerial photograph

One of the most exciting ways of studying Britain's history is to go up in an aeroplane and look at the ground from the air. Only then can you see that the Roman fort at Housesteads (see page 30) is shaped like a playing-card with rounded corners. Similar forts have been discovered in many other parts of Britain, particularly along the length of Hadrian's Wall.

Aerial photographs can sometimes reveal things which people on the ground are unable to detect, such as the course of an old road. This is shown in the aerial photograph below. Look at this carefully and then compare it with the map.

1. How can you tell that the photo shows the long-abandoned town of Silchester?

2. What makes the position of the old town walls of Silchester stand out clearly today when seen from the air?

3. The camera in the aeroplane was *not* pointing north. Look closely at the shape of the town in the photograph and at the shape of the town shown on the plan. In which direction was the camera pointing?

4. A modern road can be clearly seen cutting diagonally across the town. Does it follow the same line as a Roman road or street?

5. Make a tracing of Silchester *from the aerial photograph* and mark on it the position of the streets you can pick out in the photograph. Mark and name the approximate position of each of the following : the North, East, South and West Gates; the Forum; the inn; the public baths; the temples; the amphitheatre.

Town life

One of the most remarkable finds at Pompeii was the discovery of a large number of writings on the walls of the town. Some are trade signs indicating a fruit or cake seller. For instance, you can find out where the best fish sauce was sold in Pompeii in A.D. 79 or read about the innkeeper who served bad wine. Signs tell the stranger to beware of the dog (*cave canem* in Latin, the Roman language). Even the results of contests between gladiators in the amphitheatre were written up like football results:

'Fabius, veteran of 9 fights   KILLED
    versus
Astus, veteran of 14 fights   WON
Cycnus, veteran of 8 fights   WON
    versus
Atticus, veteran of 14 fights   REPRIEVED'

We can also learn a lot about everyday life in a typical Roman town from the poems, stories and descriptions written by Roman authors. One writer called Juvenal complained that he couldn't sleep at night for the noise of cart wheels in the narrow streets of Rome and the bad language of the drivers caught in a traffic jam. When he walked through the crowded streets during the day he was:

'blocked by the crowd in front, while those behind pushed and shoved. One bangs me with an elbow, another strikes me with a stick and yet another with a jar of wine. My legs are splattered with mud and a soldier's boots stamp on my toes.'

Stone carvings like those below show us what Roman shops looked like. In Pompeii and Herculaneum, visitors can even enter the shops themselves. In one shop, remains of different foods were found 1900 years after they had been put out on display on the counter.

History skill : looking at pictures

What types of shops are shown in the two photographs? Write one or two sentences to describe the goods on sale in each shop. How do these shops differ from their modern equivalents? Draw your own picture of a Roman street. Show shops like these. Use the details on the last few pages to help you picture what everyday life was like in a Roman town.

Carvings showing Roman shops

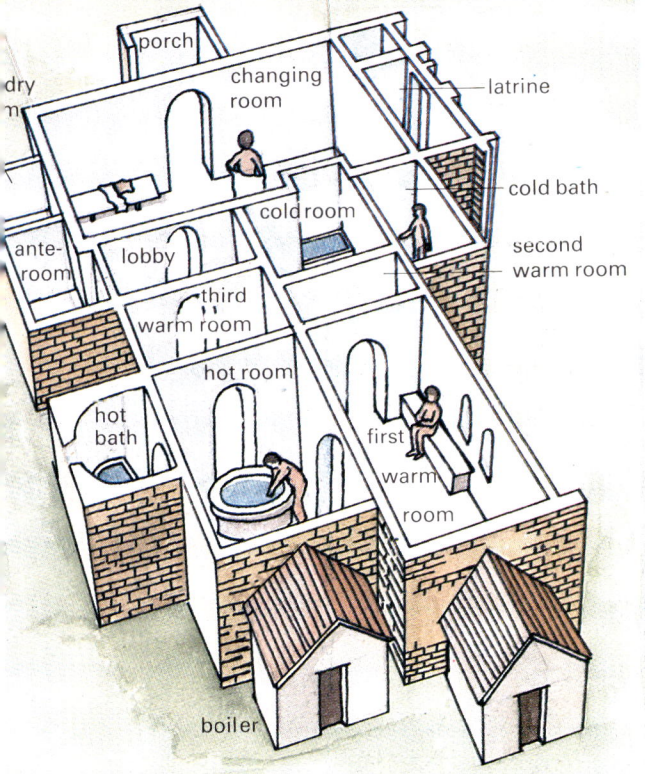

Roman baths

The great Roman bath at Bath in Avon

At the baths

The photograph (right) shows the most famous Roman bath-house in Britain.

● What features in this picture might suggest it had been built by the Romans?

The bird's-eye view of a bath-house above will help you to picture what the great bath looked like in Roman times. As you can see, the bather first undressed in the changing rooms. There were lockers for his or her clothes. There were usually separate bathing times for men and women. The bather could exercise and then enter the different rooms which varied from a hot steam room to the cold room. There were hot baths, cold baths and rest rooms. Bathers usually finished by having a massage. The masseur poured oil on to the bather's body and used a curved tool, called a strigil, to remove it. The Romans had no soap, so this was an excellent way of getting clean.

● Draw a plan of the bath-house above. Write the name of each room on your plan.

In Roman times there was a huge curved roof over the great bath at Bath in order to keep the heat in. The bath is always filled with warm spring water which bubbles to the surface at a temperature of 49°C.

● Draw or paint a picture of the great bath as it might have looked in Roman times.

Bath-houses like this were to be seen in private villas, and in military forts, as well as in the towns. The Romans went to the baths for company as well as cleanliness. They played games there, talked to their friends and relaxed in the hot and cold rooms. So even at Hadrian's Wall in the middle of winter, soldiers could come off duty, after patrolling the bleak moorlands, and enjoy the comfort and luxury of a hot bath.

History skill : discovering the past
Draw up a list of the things which might be found at the site of an excavation, which might lead you to think you had discovered the remains of a Roman bath-house.

8. Transport

Travel in prehistoric times

Very few finds have been made to show how prehistoric people travelled. Iron Age warriors were sometimes buried with their chariots or carts, so we know that wheeled traffic would have been seen on the paths of Iron Age Britain. One or two prehistoric boats have been discovered as well, such as a dugout boat (or hollowed-out tree trunk), nearly 3000 years old, which was found in Lincolnshire. A visitor to prehistoric Britain said that the Britons sailed the seas in boats made from animal skins. This is thought to refer to coracles. These were round boats made from skins which were used until recent times in Wales.

Even though it is difficult to know exactly how the people of prehistoric Britain travelled, we can be certain that they did. Bronze swords from south Germany, Austria and Switzerland have been found in the bed of the river Thames. They were made in the period from 1000 B.C. to 650 B.C.

● What does this tell you about prehistoric travel? Look at a map and work out a possible route from Austria and Switzerland to the river Thames.

Prehistoric trackways
The prehistoric peoples did not build roads. Instead, merchants and traders probably followed well-worn paths (called trackways). One of the most famous of these trackways is the Ridgeway route which can still be followed today across the chalk downs of Berkshire and Wiltshire. The valleys and plains of England at that time were often marshy and thickly forested. So it was quicker to travel across the hills where there were fewer trees.

Peddars Way in Norfolk is a trackway which traders may have followed in prehistoric times. It passed within about 10km of the flint mines at Grimes Graves in Norfolk, so it may even have been used by flint traders over 4500 years ago.

Trade in prehistoric times in the British Isles

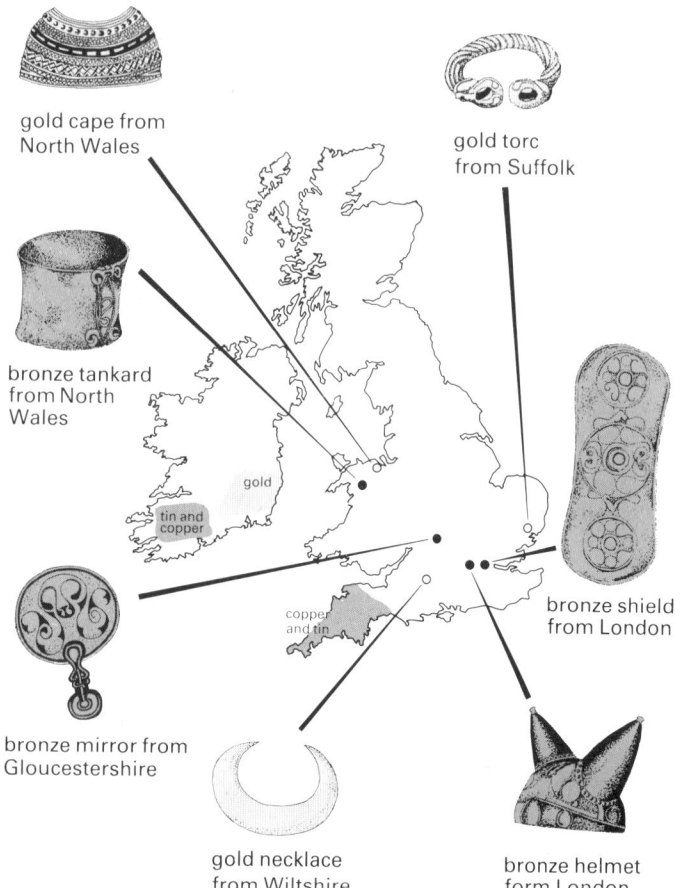

gold cape from North Wales

gold torc from Suffolk

bronze tankard from North Wales

gold

tin and copper

copper and tin

bronze shield from London

bronze mirror from Gloucestershire

gold necklace from Wiltshire

bronze helmet form London

History skill : finding out from a map
Look at the map showing where a number of gold and bronze objects have been found in the British Isles. The map also shows the only important places where gold, copper and tin were found in prehistoric Britain. Molten copper and tin together make bronze.

What does this map tell you about transport in prehistoric Britain?

Roman port in Britain

Roman building in Dover

A Roman port

We don't have to guess what Roman ships looked like. The picture of a Roman port in Britain, which you can see in the picture, has been drawn with the help of Roman carvings and pictures as a guide. We can also get evidence from the sea itself. Sunken ships are as useful as the objects which have been found in the ground by archaeologists.

In 1962, the remains of a Roman merchant ship about 20m long were discovered lying in the mud of the Thames near Blackfriars Bridge in London. We know it was Roman because a Roman coin from about A.D. 88 had been wedged under the mast for luck, and there were several pieces of Roman pottery on board. The ship was carrying building stone from Kent to London.

In Roman times the Thames would have been very busy, as ships brought goods from various parts of the Roman Empire to London. There was wine from Germany carried in huge pots called amphorae. There was pottery from Gaul (now France) and olive oil from Spain. The Roman ports in Britain were also used to ship products from Britain to Rome. Britain was a Roman colony and

History skill : imagining the past
Imagine you are a Roman sailor on your first journey from Rome to Britain. Write two or three sentences for a letter home to Rome, describing the arrival of your ship in Dover harbour at night. The picture above will help you to describe the scene at the dockside.

the Romans expected it to help supply some of the goods which were needed in Rome. We know this from the descriptions of Roman writers.

The writer Tacitus said 'Britain produces gold, silver and other metals, so it was well worth taking'. Slaves, skins, lead, tin, baskets and woollen cloth were among the many products which were taken to Rome.

● The photograph shows an unusual Roman building on the rocky headland overlooking the port of Dover. A flaming torch on the top of this building could have been seen for many kilometres across the English Channel. In Roman times it was nearly twice as tall as this. A matching building stood on the other side of the harbour. What do you think these buildings were used for?

41

Roman road at Wheeldale Moor, North Yorkshire

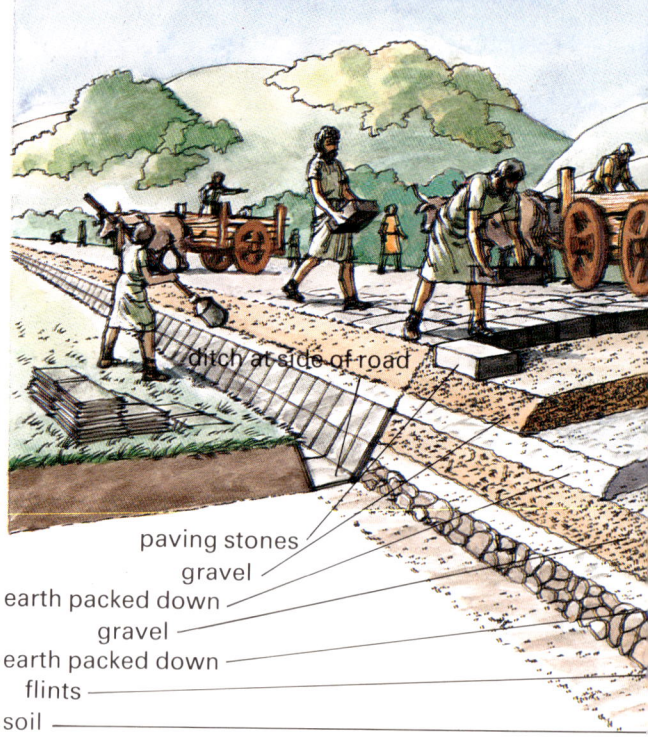

ditch at side of road

paving stones
gravel
earth packed down
gravel
earth packed down
flints
soil

Constructing a Roman road

A Roman road

The road you can see in the photograph was built about 1900 years ago on Wheeldale Moor near Scarborough in Yorkshire. The picture shows how the Romans constructed a road like this. In Roman times the Wheeldale Moor road would have been covered with fine gravel, which the traffic on the road would have pressed down to make a firm, smooth surface.

● What do you think has happened to the gravel which used to cover the road?
● What was the purpose of the ditch on the left in the photograph? Why is the level of the road higher than that of the surrounding moorland? Why was the surface of a Roman road slightly curved, so that both sides dipped gently towards the ditches on either side?
● Write two or three sentences to say how a Roman road was built.
● The Romans built about 10 000km of roads in Britain, but the Wheeldale Moor stretch is one of the few remaining Roman road surfaces still to be seen. What do you

thinks has happened to the other 9990km or so of road?

Many modern roads follow the same course as the old Roman roads. Sometimes this is because the only sensible route along the side of the valley is the one which the Romans followed nearly 2000 years ago. The Romans liked to build their roads as straight as possible. As you have already seen, the streets in the towns were straight and crossed each other at right angles. When the Romans built their roads in Britain, they didn't have to worry about who owned the land. They could build the road in a straight line and so cut down the amount of building material needed and the travelling time taken once the road was built. Later road builders often had to curve their roads to avoid castles, abbeys, farms, fields and forests. Their roads were rarely straight.

Today the fact that a stretch of modern road is very straight is a useful clue which suggests that it might possibly be a part of an old Roman road. If there is a road like this in your home area, it will probably be marked as a ROMAN ROAD on a local map.

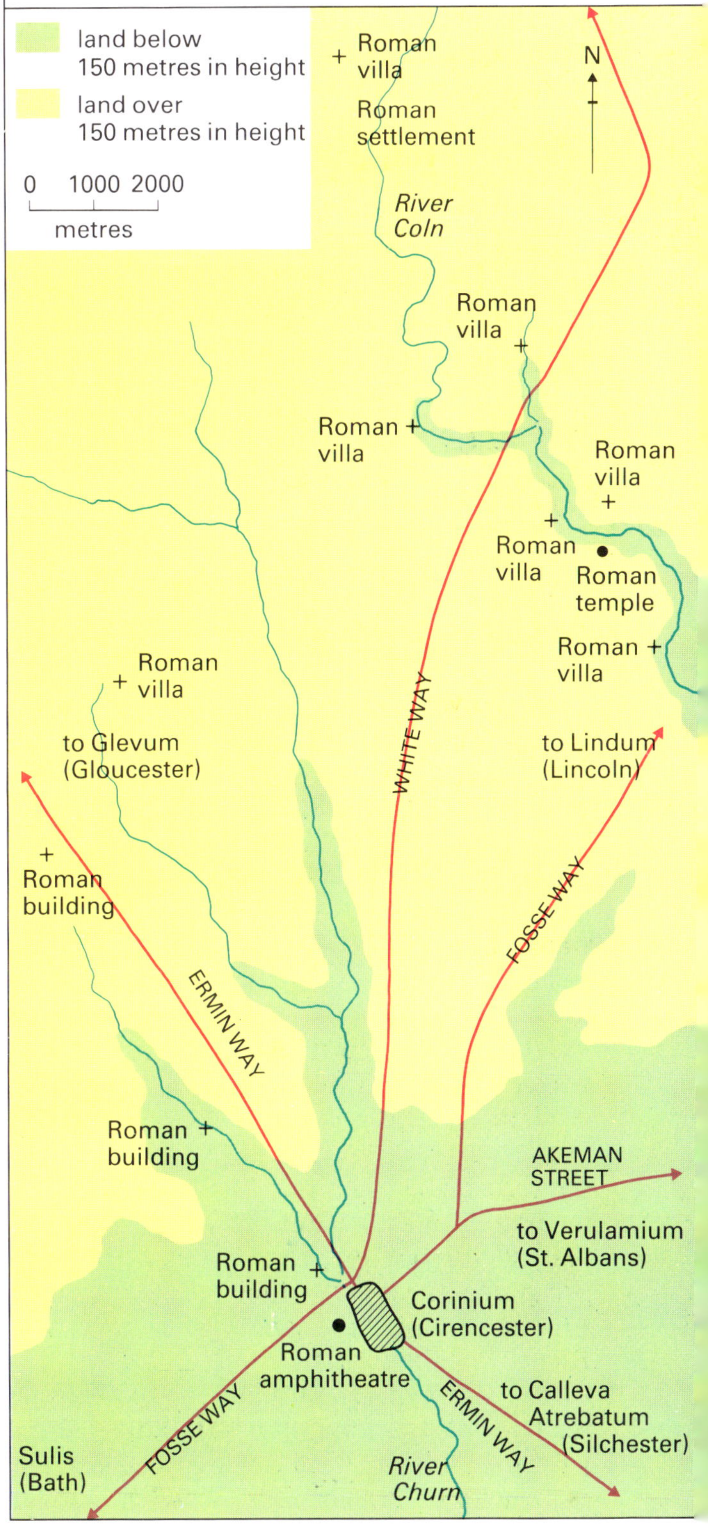

History skill : finding out from a map

This map shows the district close to Cirencester in Gloucestershire. It has been drawn from a modern map of the area. Cirencester was known as Corinium, and it was the second largest town in Roman Britain. Look at the map carefully and answer these questions.

1. How many Roman roads met in or close to Cirencester? To which other important Roman towns was Cirencester directly connected by road? Why are large towns almost always road junctions?

2. How many villas or other Roman buildings are shown on the map? How many of these are situated close to a river? How many are situated within about 3km of a Roman road?

3. Write two or three sentences to say what you have found out from the map.

4. Write down two or three reasons which help to explain why Corinium was an important town in Roman Britain.

5. See if you can find a map of your home area. Draw a map like the one on this page. Mark in the sites of Roman villas, forts, camps, temples, amphitheatres and settlements. Draw in the course of any Roman roads shown on the map. What facts can you find out about the Roman settlement of your area?

Map of the district close to the Roman city of Corinium (Cirencester)

land below 150 metres in height

land over 150 metres in height

0 1000 2000
metres

N

Roman villa

Roman settlement

River Coln

Roman villa

Roman villa

Roman villa

Roman villa

Roman temple

Roman villa

Roman villa

to Lindum (Lincoln)

WHITE WAY

FOSSE WAY

Roman building

to Glevum (Gloucester)

ERMIN WAY

Roman building

AKEMAN STREET

to Verulamium (St. Albans)

Roman building

Corinium (Cirencester)

Roman amphitheatre

to Calleva Atrebatum (Silchester)

ERMIN WAY

FOSSE WAY

Sulis (Bath)

River Churn

43

9. Farming

Celtic fields

Look at the photograph. This view from the air shows the outline of a number of small fields. They were farmed in prehistoric times and are called Celtic Fields. They are named after the Celts who were the most important of the Iron Age people who lived in Britain before the Roman conquest. In actual fact, many Celtic fields may be much older than this. Some may go back to the time of the Bronze Age farmers over 3000 years ago.

Remains of the work of the Bronze Age farmers have been found in several different places, from the hut circles at Grimspound on Dartmoor to the round beehive huts of the farmers who settled at Itford Hill in Sussex over 3000 years ago. You can see an imaginary picture of one of their villages on page 25.

In about 1000 B.C. Bronze Age farmers first started to use a light wooden plough which was called the ard. It was pulled by oxen and it helped these farmers to cultivate the squarish fields you can see in the photograph. With better tools and implements, they were able to improve the farming methods of the New Stone Age farmers you read about on page 10. They cultivated the land with flint hoes and reaped their corn with flint sickles. By contrast, the Bronze Age farmers of 3000 years ago were ploughing their fields with the ard and harvesting their corn with bronze sickles instead of flint.

● Roughly how many separate fields are there in the area shown in the photograph? What shape are they? Can you see the boundaries of the modern fields? On the ground it would be difficult to pick out the Celtic fields. Write a sentence to say why you think it is fairly easy to pick them out from the air.

Aerial photograph of Celtic fields near Lewes in Sussex

Aerial photographs

As you have already seen, an aerial photograph can help us to see the complete outline of a Roman fort like Housesteads. It is unmistakably a Roman fort from the air but, to most people, only a collection of ruins on the ground. An aerial photograph shows clearly the street pattern in an abandoned town like Silchester (page 37).

Discovering new sites

Aerial photographs have other uses in history as well. They sometimes reveal a pattern in fields of growing corn which no-one had thought interesting before. Archaeologists or historians may think this is a site worth investigating on the ground.

- What patterns on an aerial photograph might lead you to think of (a) a Roman road, (b) a Roman fort, (c) a Roman villa?

One reason why the aerial photograph is so good at spotting patterns like this is because it is often taken at an angle. When the sun is low in the sky, the shadows are longer than at midday. They often emphasize differences in height or of shape. Small bumps and hollows revealed in this way may later prove to be the foundations of old buildings.

Another reason why aerial photographs are good at picking out patterns is because growing crops sometimes change their colour slightly when ripening. This is especially noticeable during a long period of drought (when there is no rain). A simple explanation of why this happens is shown in the diagrams.

Why aerial photographs can pick out buried prehistoric or Roman sites which are not visible on the surface

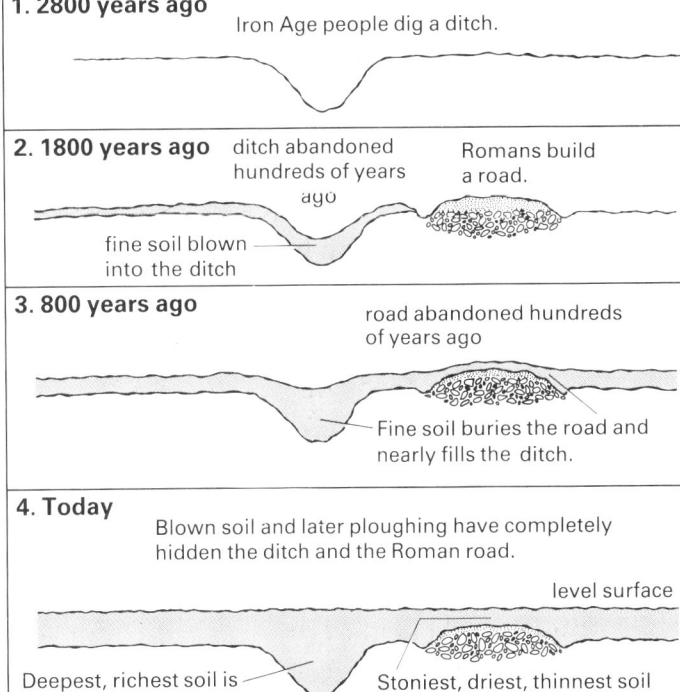

1. 2800 years ago — Iron Age people dig a ditch.

2. 1800 years ago — ditch abandoned hundreds of years ago — Romans build a road. — fine soil blown into the ditch

3. 800 years ago — road abandoned hundreds of years ago — Fine soil buries the road and nearly fills the ditch.

4. Today — Blown soil and later ploughing have completely hidden the ditch and the Roman road. — level surface — Deepest, richest soil is at the bottom of the ditch where it keeps a lot of its moisture. — Stoniest, driest, thinnest soil is above the Roman road.

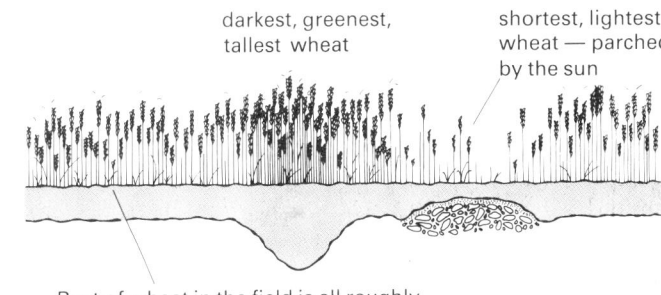

5. Today — during a long drought in the summer — darkest, greenest, tallest wheat — shortest, lightest wheat — parched by the sun — Rest of wheat in the field is all roughly the same height and colour.

History skill : using an aerial photograph

Where does the wheat grow tallest? Why? Where does it grow shortest? Why? What other differences are there?

How does an aerial photograph pick out the differences in height between the wheat growing over the ditch and the wheat growing over the road? How does it pick out the differences in colour between the ordinary wheat in the field, the wheat growing over the ditch and the wheat growing over the road?

What would you expect to see in an aerial photograph of the Iron Age ditch and Roman road if it was taken during a period of drought?

The Iron Age farm at Butser in Hampshire

An Iron Age farm

This is the Iron Age farm at Butser in Hampshire, which you also saw in the photograph on pages 28–29. How the Iron Age people lived and farmed has interested many people. The B.B.C. built its own Iron Age hut with the labour of a group of volunteers. They lived there for a year and farmed the land with Iron Age implements and methods.

The Iron Age farm at Butser was also built as part of a practical experiment to see how the Iron Age people farmed their land. By testing tools and implements in this way, scientists are able to throw new light on the discoveries which have been made on the sites of actual Iron Age farming villages.

We also know something about farming in Britain at this time from the descriptions written by people who were living in Rome and who had either visited Britain or heard tales from travellers and traders. You can read some of these accounts if you turn back to page 17.

● Write a brief description of Iron Age farming in Britain, using the written descriptions on page 17 as your only source of information.
● How does the Iron Age farm at Butser in Hampshire compare with the descriptions of British farming written by Pytheas, Strabo, Diodorus and Julius Caesar?

History skill : making comparisons
The pictures show what it may have been like to spend a year in an Iron Age village. In what ways are these activities similar to those to be seen on a British farm today? In what ways are they different?

A year on an Iron Age farm

Spring

ploughing the fields

lambing-time

Summer

weeding the corn by hoeing

shearing the sheep

making hay

Autumn

threshing corn

harvesting corn with iron sickles

using a flail to beat the corn

winnowing the grain by throwing it in the air and letting the wind blow away the chaff

using a quern to grind corn into flour

pots holding flour

storing grain in underground pits

Winter

feeding cattle in compound

collecting wood for fire

killing pigs for meat

Farming in Roman times

What we know about Roman farms in Britain comes mainly from the archaeological discoveries which have been made at villas in southern England. This was where the best farmland was situated and where the climate was most suitable for growing corn. It was also closest to the main Roman towns and the ports and harbours on the south coast.

We can also get some information from pictures, stone carvings, poems and stories from Rome itself. These can all help to build up a picture of life in the countryside in Roman Britain. The photograph opposite shows a bronze statue of a farmer at work, which was found at Piercebridge in County Durham.

● What farming activity does the statue show? What animals are shown?

The other pictures on these pages have been partly based on carvings and paintings which have been found in Rome and in other parts of the Roman Empire. They are also partly based on the results of archaeological discoveries. Examine these pictures carefully.

● How did ordinary British farmers live and work during the period of the Roman conquest? Was their life very different from that of the Iron Age farmers? Were Roman farming methods much different from those of the Iron Age?
● Write an imaginary description of a visit to a Roman farm about 1800 years ago. Describe one of the important farming activities of the year, such as ploughing the fields or harvest-time.
● Write one or two sentences to say what you think a Neolithic farmer would have noticed first of all on a visit to a farm in Britain in about A.D. 200.

Farming in Roman Britain

48

Farming in Roman Britain

Museum displays

Many museums throughout Britain contain finds which tell us a lot about Roman farming methods. Look at this list of objects from a display in the Museum of London. Most of these were discovered in the bed of a stream which used to flow near the Bank of England in the heart of the City of London.

— a cheese press;
— a honey pot;
— an iron spade;
— a goad — a long stick with a spike on the end, which was used to drive cattle;
— iron teeth from a wooden rake;
— an iron sickle;
— a pruning hook;
— an iron hoe;
— an iron ploughshare

In a similar display in the Castle Museum in Norwich you can see:

— a quern for grinding corn, which was probably powered by a donkey walking round and round;
— a wooden spade with the edges of the blade covered with an iron sheath.

History skill: finding out from archaeological discoveries

Answer the questions which follow, using only the information you can get by studying the objects on display in the two museums.

1. How do we know the farmers of Roman Britain grew corn? List the discoveries which provide clues to the different farming activities involved.
2. How do we know they milked their animals?
3. Excavations at the luxurious Roman villa at Fishbourne show that there were large gardens there. As you have seen on page 33, the Roman writer Pliny was proud of his garden. What do these museum finds tell you about Roman gardeners over 1800 years ago?
4. Make a list of the products which these discoveries tell us came from farms in Roman Britain.

If you visit a local museum, go to the displays of Roman discoveries. Make a similar list of finds which provide clues telling us about Roman farms and farming methods.

10. Industry

A prehistoric flint mine

You have already seen that there was a trade in flints in the prehistoric period. The best flints were well worth looking for, since they were much in demand for use as axeheads, knives and scrapers. We know this because archaeologists have excavated deep pits, or mines, at Grimes Graves in Norfolk. These show that flint miners were working up to 12 metres below ground level extracting flints. They dug galleries (or tunnels) to get at the flints. What is remarkable is that this prehistoric flint mining industry was active over 4500 years ago.

The photograph on the right shows one of the pits which these miners dug in about 2500 B.C. Today it looks just like a deep hollow in the ground which has been filled with sand and lumps of chalk. In fact this is the rubble which was put there when the pit was abandoned. When the flint miners dug a hole (or pit shaft) about 12 metres deep, they had to get rid of the earth and soil and stones they came across. So these were put in the

Prehistoric flint mine at Grimes Graves in Norfolk

Mining flints at Grimes Graves, Norfolk

old pit from which the flints had all been taken. Today Grimes Graves is an uneven area of wasteland, with hummocks and hollows marking the position of as many as 300 old flint mines.

Some of these pits have been excavated. Visitors to the site today can go down to the bottom of the pit shown in the photograph on the left. The galleries have been covered with metal grilles to stop foolhardy people tampering with the tunnels leading from the pit shaft.

The picture has been drawn using some of the evidence which tells us about the way these flint workers mined the flints. Deer antlers have been found amongst the rubble. These were obviously used as pick axes to remove flints stuck in the rock face. A lamp made from a piece of chalk was also found there, together with carvings made by the miners. Animal bones may have been used as spades or levers.

Underground galleries at Grimes Graves, Norfolk

Miners at work

It is dark at the bottom of the mine shafts. Today, electric light enables visitors to see the galleries. Imagine the same scene 4500 years ago. The only light the miners would have had came from chalk lamps. These were hollowed-out stones filled with animal fat.

We have no idea how the miners got down the pit shaft to go to work, nor do we know how the heavy flints were raised to the surface. It would have been impossible to build a set of steps at the side of the pit. So archaeologists think these miners used rope ladders with wooden steps tied together with animal thongs. You can see how the artist has shown this in the picture.

Today, when coal is mined in a colliery, the coal is processed on the surface of the mine. This means it is washed to get rid of the dirt and then graded into different types of coal. Something like this happened at the Neolithic flint mine 4500 years ago. Workmen, whom we call flint knappers, shaped the raw flints into axeheads. They did this by chipping off flakes of flint. It was a skilled task, since a poor flint knapper could easily waste a good flint by chipping off too big a flake.

We know these flint knappers worked on the surface, because piles of waste flakes and partly completed flint axes have been discovered on the ground above the level of the pit shafts.

History skill : writing a description

Write a description of the way in which flints were mined at Grimes Graves under these separate headings:

1. How the pits were dug.
2. The tools and implements the miners used to get down the pit shaft and to extract the flints.
3. How the flints were taken to the surface and turned into flint axes.

sand

boulder clay

soft chalk

hard chalk

flint nodules

flint nodules

Prehistoric industries

The pictures on these pages show three of the four most important industries in prehistoric Britain.

● What were these four industries? Name a product from each industry. Write a sentence to say whether the industry is still important today.

Pottery industries

The Neolithic farmers are believed to have been the first people in Britain to use pottery. Pottery is made from wet clay. The early potters moulded it into shape with their fingers and then 'fired' it to bake the clay hard. Nowadays baking is done in an electric kiln. At first the clay pots were probably baked by being placed at the side of an open fire.

In the Neolithic and Bronze Age periods, the pottery was coarser and not as smooth as the pottery made in the Iron Age and by the Romans. Improvements came about 2100 years ago when the Iron Age potters began to use the potter's wheel. This is a wheel which allows a clay ball to be turned round and round quickly. As the wheel revolves, the potter shapes the clay into a bowl or jug. The Iron Age and Roman potters also used better kilns. This meant that their pots were baked at higher temperatures and this made them harder and of better quality than those of the Neolithic potters.

● How does this fact help archaeologists with their work?

The potters who worked in a particular place and at a particular period of time usually made their pots in the same style. These were usually of a similar thickness and shape. Often they had similar decorations. So even though today the only evidence of this pottery may be tiny fragments (called sherds), they are still of great value to archaeologists. They tell us much more about a prehistoric site then just the fact that the people used pots.

● Why is the fact that pottery is fragile but difficult to destroy a godsend to archaeologists? Why are the sherds so valuable? How can pottery help to say how old a site is and who lived there?

History skill : using your imagination

How do you think the prehistoric people first discovered that pottery could be made from clay and that cloth could be made by weaving strands of wool? Write an imaginary account of the ways in which you think these industries first began.

Metal industries

In the Bronze Age people began to use metal ornaments, tools and weapons. We know this because gold necklaces, copper bowls and bronze knives have been found.

The idea of using copper and bronze instead of flint probably came from Europe. A lump of copper ore may have softened up in the hot charcoal embers of a fire fanned by a high wind. Imagine the surprise of the people who first discovered that it could be moulded into shape. Later they discovered that the copper shape had become hard when the metal cooled.

Copper ore is often found near tin ore, so by accident the Bronze Age smiths may have discovered that a mixture of tin and copper made a stronger metal.

● What is that 'mixed' metal called?

To make metal tools, the bronzesmiths had to heat the metal to high temperatures. They did this by building small furnaces from stone and clay and using bellows to force a draught through the charcoal embers inside.

● How do you think they shaped the red-hot metal into tools, ornaments and weapons?

It is easy to think of prehistoric people as primitive because they had no written language and left no record of their famous men and women. But if you look in a museum at the axes, knives and ornaments the prehistoric craftsmen made, you will be surprised to see the high standard of their workmanship.

Cloth industries

Weaving also became an important industry during the Bronze Age and Iron Age. We know this because fragments of woollen cloth and a number of loom weights have been found. Prehistoric weavers used vertical looms in which the warp threads (those which hang down) were kept stretched by hanging heavy loom weights on the ends.

● In what ways were the prehistoric industries of mining, pottery, metal-working and weaving different from those same industries today?

Roman industries

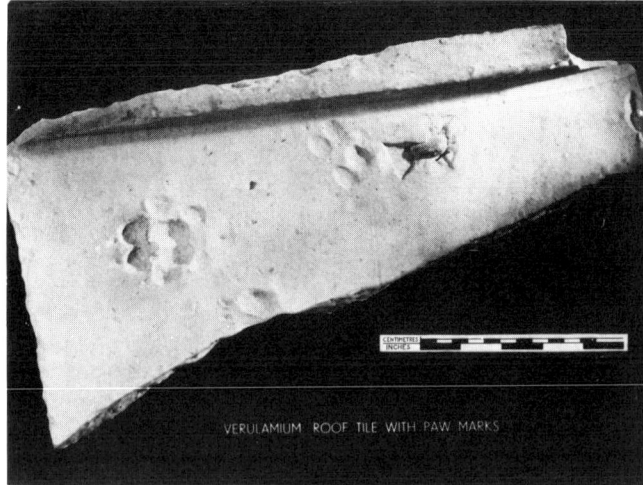

VERULAMIUM ROOF TILE WITH PAW MARKS

Roof tile in the Roman museum in St Albans

If you ever visit a museum with a good collection of Roman tools and implements, you may be surprised to see how many of them resemble the same sort of implements we use today. You may see needles, hammers, nails, butcher's knives, axes and many other everyday tools and implements.

The picture opposite has been drawn using information from what we know about workshops in Pompeii, and partly from studying the many Roman tools and implements which have been discovered in Britain. All the implements shown in the picture can be seen in museums today.

● Write down the names of the tools you can identify.
● What type of workshop is this? How is it similar to the workshop of a keen amateur today or the workshop in your school used for making similar products? How is it different?

The streets of a Roman town were loud with the sounds of hammering and banging from scores of small workshops like this. Most industries were carried on in small workshops rather than in factories. However, some woollen cloth may have been woven in the Imperial Weaving Sheds in Winchester and stained in the dyeing works at nearby Silchester. The remains of fulling mills, where woollen cloth was scoured and cleaned, have also been discovered at Chcdworth in Gloucestershire and Darenth in Kent.

Mining

The Romans were very efficient at organising the building of an amphitheatre or road, so it would not be surprising if their mines were run just as efficiently. They mined lead in the Pennines in northern England and in the Mendips in the West Country. They extracted gold at Dolaucothi in south Wales and mined tin ore in Cornwall. Iron mines and iron works were to be seen in Kent and in the Midlands.

They used wood and charcoal for most of their fuel, but they also made use of coal as well. There is no coalfield in Wiltshire, yet coal has been found on Roman sites there. One of their main sources of power came from water. The discovery of large grindstones in the bed of the Wallbrook, one of the streams flowing into the Thames, shows there was a water-mill there in Roman times. It was probably used for grinding corn.

Other industries

Some of the Roman industries were very advanced. Window glass, for instance, was used hundreds of years before it again became a common feature of houses in Britain (from the time of Queen Elizabeth I). Pottery was often stamped with the name of the potter, such as the mixing bowl in the Museum of London which carried the name of a potter called Doinus who made it in about A.D. 100.

We can even learn what people thought about their work. A London brickmaker told tales on a fellow worker by writing on a wall 'Austalis has been going off on his own every day for the past fortnight'.

Facts about these industries came from many parts of Britain. A pottery kiln which was found in Norfolk had a stoke-hole, a flue to create a draught, an area for the furnace and a platform forming the oven floor where the pots were baked. On a pot found at Corbridge in Northumberland there is a picture showing the god of blacksmiths, holding a hammer in one hand and a pair of tongs in the other. An anvil can be seen in the background.

11. Everyday life

A prehistoric funeral

It may seem odd, but much of what we know about everyday life in prehistoric times comes from studying burial mounds like the long barrow at West Kennet in Wiltshire. You can see it in the photographs on this page and on page 10.

• Look at these photographs carefully. Imagine you are an archaeologist seeing these burial chambers for the first time. Write or tape a report describing what you can see. Give an estimate of the size of the stones the New Stone Age people used when building this tomb.

Burial methods differed among the various peoples who lived in prehistoric times. Some of the Iron Age people who lived about 2000 years ago buried their warrior chiefs alongside their weapons, clothes, ornaments and chariots. These people also left food and drink which they thought the dead would need in their life after death.

Some of the Bronze Age tribes, who lived over 3000 years ago, cremated their dead. They enclosed the ashes in urns shaped like buckets, which they buried underground. Other Bronze Age peoples, who lived from about 4000 to 3500 years ago, buried their dead beneath round barrows. These are usually smaller than the Neolithic long barrows. Round barrows usually contained the remains of only one person. Those shaped like a disc usually contained the body of a woman, and those shaped like a bell the body of a man.

The oldest burial places are those of the Neolithic farmers who lived from about 6500 to 4000 years ago. They built the chambered tomb and long barrow at West Kennet, and intended it as the last resting place for a number of people. We know this because archaeologists have discovered the remains of about 46 people there.

Entrance to the chambered tomb at West Kennet, Wiltshire

A Neolithic burial scene about 4500 years ago

At West Kennet it is not hard to imagine a scene something like the one shown in the picture. This shows a burial ceremony about 4500 years ago. (The stone slabs covering the burial chamber have been left out by the artist to show the inside.)

● Name *five* things which you would like to know about the everyday life of the Neolithic peoples. Write against each of the items on your list the names of any archaeological discoveries which you think might help to answer your questions.

History skill : looking at the evidence

A number of other pieces of information are known about the long barrow at West Kennet. Look at this list of clues and then answer the questions which follow.

☆ At least 12 of the skeletons are the remains of children, including seven infants and four babies.

☆ The burials took place over a period of many years — perhaps as long as 500 years or more.

☆ We know that a local doctor removed many human bones from the barrow in 1685. He said he used them to make a 'medicine'.

☆ Neolithic pottery was discovered among the remains — some of it at least 4500 years old.

☆ We know that some of the skeletons are not complete and that many skulls are missing.

☆ An arrowhead was found near the skeleton of one man.

Look at the statements below. Write a sentence for each of these statements, giving one or two facts which show why the experts are able to know this.

1. The tomb was in use in about 2500 B.C.
2. More than 46 people were originally buried there — perhaps a lot more.
3. The Neolithic people who built this tomb probably believed in a life after death.
4. The tomb may have been used as the burial place for all the members of a family over a period of many years.
5. Children often died young in those days, at a time when life was hard and there were no nurses or doctors.
6. The Neolithic people had leaders who were good at organizing things.

57

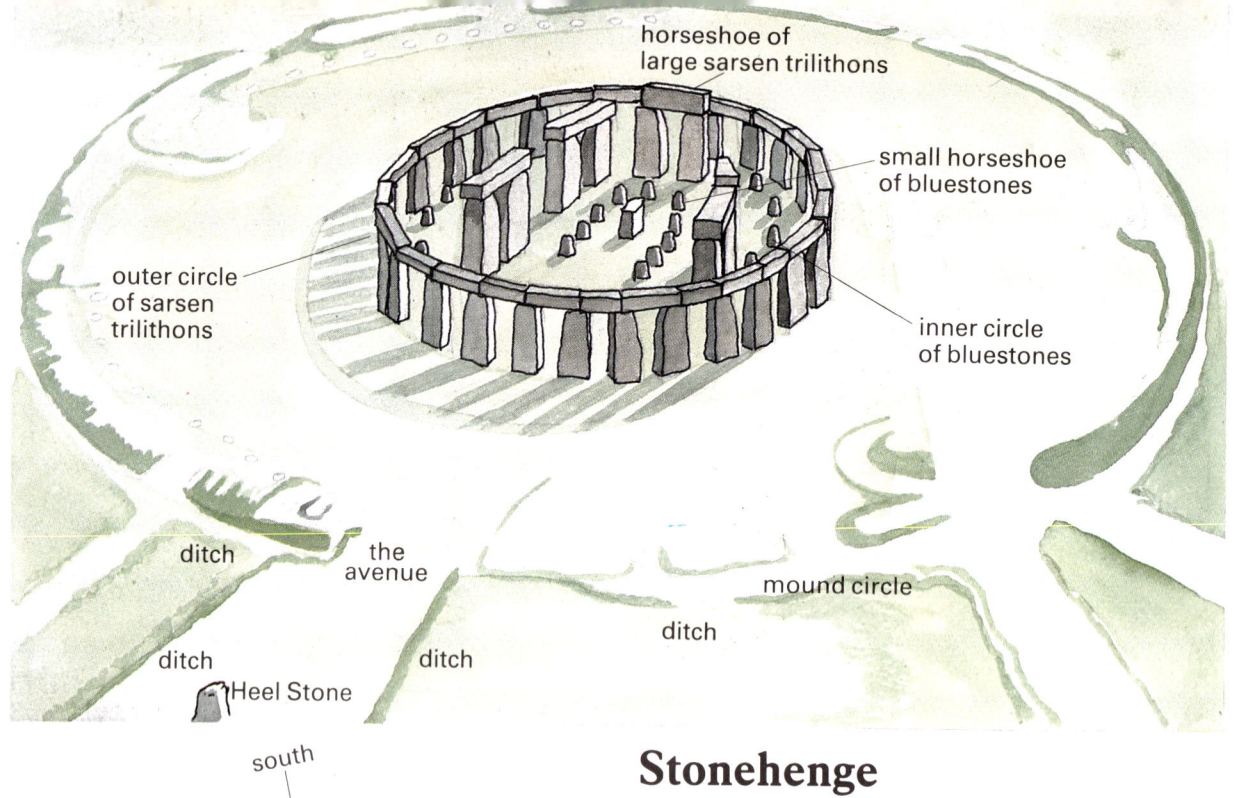

horseshoe of large sarsen trilithons

small horseshoe of bluestones

outer circle of sarsen trilithons

inner circle of bluestones

ditch

the avenue

mound circle

ditch

ditch

ditch

Heel Stone

south

east — west

north

Stonehenge

The picture map shows Stonehenge as it probably looked over 3000 years ago during the Bronze Age. As you can see, the two horseshoes of stones in the middle of the two circles point straight down the avenue towards the Heel Stone, which stands some distance away.

Some experts believe that Stonehenge was a kind of prehistoric astronomical observatory. It may have been used to observe the movement of the sun, moon, planets and stars. There were no clocks or calendars then, but farmers knew that the daily period of darkness was much longer in the colder part of the year than in the warmer. They knew too that the reason for these differences was due to the position of the sun in the sky.

● As you know, the earth rotates on its axis once every 24 hours. This means that in Britain the sun is due north at 12.00 midnight and due south at 12.00 midday. Work out from these facts where the sun will appear to be at 6.00 a.m. and 6.00 p.m. When will the sun be north-east (halfway between north and east)?

History skill : compass directions on a map

Look at the picture map carefully.
1. If you stood in the middle of the horseshoe of stones and looked down the avenue towards the Heel Stone, would you be facing (a) north, (b) east, (c) just over halfway between north and east, (d) south-east (roughly halfway between south and east)?
2. The earliest time in the day when the sun rises is on Midsummer Day, 21 June — the longest day of the year. At Stonehenge this happens at about 3.50 a.m. (or 4.50 a.m. nowadays, since we put the clocks on one hour during summer time). From which direction will the sun appear at sunrise at Stonehenge on Midsummer Day?
3. In which direction will the shadow of the Heel Stone point at sunrise on Midsummer Day?

Stonehenge in Wiltshire

The Heel Stone seen through the arch of a trilithon at Stonehenge

Building Stonehenge

Stonehenge was built over a period of about a thousand years from 2200 B.C. to 1200 B.C. It is made up of sarsen stones and bluestones. The sarsen stones are huge blocks of sandstone which were found on the Wiltshire downlands some distance away from Stonehenge. Archaeologists think they may have been rolled there on logs. You can picture this for yourself if you rest a book on top of six pencils. The book can be easily moved forward on these rollers. Imagine doing the same thing with stones weighing as much as 30 tonnes apiece! The bluestones come from a rock which is only found a long distance away in Wales. It may have been quarried by prehistoric stone workers and taken to Stonehenge on rafts and overland. Other experts believe the stones may have been lying close to Stonehenge, having been carried there by glaciers during the Ice Age.

One of the miracles of Stonehenge is the way in which the upright stones were shaped with stone hammers. Knobs of stone were left upstanding on each of the huge blocks of stone which form the uprights in the trilithons. Trilithon simply means 'three stones'. This is the arrangement of stones you can see in the photograph. Two stones stand upright a short distance apart, and a third stone (called the lintel stone) lies on top. These lintel stones were shaped so that they had holes underneath which matched the tenons on the uprights.

● What was the builders' reason for shaping the stones like this?

The edges of the lintel stones were also shaped so that they curved gently. When all the lintel stones were placed in position, this curving created a perfect circle.

● Look at the photograph on the left. Use the height of the people (roughly 1.6 metres) to estimate the height of the tall upright stone on the left.
● How can you tell that the stones of the trilithon in the middle were shaped by stonemasons?
● Draw a simple sketch of the stones shown in the photograph. Label a tenon, lintel stone and trilithon.
● How do you think the trilithons were erected? How did the builders raise the stones?

Religion in the Iron Age

When Julius Caesar wrote the history of his expedition against the Gauls and Britons, he had this to say about the Druids.

'They are in charge of the religion and control the sacrifices. They teach the young men and act as judges when crimes are committed or if there is a quarrel over property. The Druids are led by one man. They hold a meeting every year in a sacred place.'

● Are there any modern equivalents of the Druids?

Much of what we know about the Druids and their religion comes from Roman writings like this. Unfortunately, it isn't always easy to say whether the writers were telling the truth or whether they were exaggerating.

Scene showing a sacrifice on a bowl found in Denmark

History skill : weighing up the evidence
Study the information below.
1. A writer called Diodorus Siculus said that the Druids were always present when the Britons made sacrifices.

'The soothsayers practise a strange and incredible ceremony. Having chosen a victim for sacrifice, they stab him with a knife and foretell the future from the way he falls and the flowing of his blood.'

2. The skeleton of a woman was found in a pit below the foundations of the ramparts at Maiden Castle hill fort. It is thought she may have been sacrificed in order to bring good luck to the people who were to live in the fort. Skeletons with knife marks on them or severed limbs have been found at other Iron Age sites.
3. A sacred silver bowl used by Iron Age people about 2100 years ago was found in a bog in Denmark. As you can see, it has a scene depicting a sacrifice on the side.

Do you think this extra evidence makes Diodorus's account more or less likely to be true? Does the picture on the Danish bowl help to prove that Iron Age people in Britain also conducted sacrifices? Are there any other possible explanations for the mutilated skeletons or the picture of a sacrifice on a bowl? What further facts might help you to believe or disbelieve the Roman writers? Would you need to know whether they had ever been to Britain? Does Julius Caesar's account provide reliable evidence?

Discuss this topic with your friends.

The Temple of Mithras
The photograph on page 61 shows a very unusual ruin which can be seen in Northumberland close to Hadrian's Wall. This is the Temple of Mithras at Carrawburgh. The picture (right) shows what this temple might have looked like in Roman times.

The religion of Mithraism originally came from Persia (nowadays known as Iran). It was for men only and its followers worshipped Mithras, the god of light. They had a

Temple of Mithras

high regard for bravery and courage, and tested new worshippers by making them suffer tests designed to see how strong and courageous they were. Those who were successful could take further tests and hope in time to rise to the higher grades of worshipper, such as the grade of the raven or the lion.

• Why do you think the worship of Mithras was popular with soldiers?

• Look at the pictures carefully and then answer these questions.

1. Roughly how big was the temple? Use the size of the figures to guess the approximate height, width and length of the temple.

2. Write a sentence to describe the atmosphere inside the temple. Does it resemble any place of worship you have been to?

3. What do you notice about some of the worshippers? What is odd about their appearance?

4. Make a simple tracing of the temple in the photograph. Mark in and label the position of (a) the altar where incense is burning, (b) the platform where some members of the congregation sat or stood.

5. Mark in on your tracing of the temple the approximate position of a Roman who has reached the level of the lion.

How the Temple of Mithras may have looked in Roman times

61

At play

Look at this photograph showing a mosaic found in a Roman villa. It can be seen in Hull Museum.

● What type of sport does the mosaic show?
● Write two or three sentences to describe the contestants. Write about their clothes, vehicles and their horses.

In Rome the chariot races took place in a huge stadium called the Circus Maximus. It was oval in shape and specially designed for fast chariot races. No stadiums like this have been found in Britain, but chariot races are believed to have taken place here. Mosaics like the one found in Lincolnshire would not have shown scenes like this if they weren't familiar to people living in Britain.

Amphitheatres have been discovered, however, such as those at Caerleon in South Wales, Dorchester, Silchester and Cirencester. In Rome, the Colosseum was the most famous amphitheatre. It was here that gladiators fought to the death against each other. Slaves were sometimes thrown to the wild beasts who provided barbaric entertainment for the bloodthirsty Roman crowds.

People packed the 50 000 seats in the Colosseum on the days when the 'games' were held.

It is unlikely that lions, tigers and elephants werc seen in the amphitheatres of Roman Britain. The cost of bringing them here would not have been worthwhile. Instead, wolves and bears might have been seen, together with bull-baiting and contests between gladiators. At the Roman amphitheatre in Dorchester, a room near the entrance is thought to have been used as a cage for wild animals.

History skill : studying a picture
Look at the mosaic opposite which shows scenes in a Roman amphitheatre. Write or tape an account of the 'games' using these pictures as your only source of information.
1. Which picture shows a defeated gladiator?
Why is someone holding the arm of the man standing over him?
2. How many different types of gladiator can you see? How were they armed?
3. How many different wild animals can you identify? Whom were they fighting?
4. What other entertainments could be seen in the amphitheatre?

Theatres

The Romans also built theatres where actors and actresses could perform plays. The theatre at St Albans, shown in the photograph here , is one of the rare examples of a Roman theatre in Britain. You can tell it is a theatre, since the rows of seats do not completely encircle the central arena, as in an amphitheatre. In fact, the word *amphitheatre* simply means a theatre on both sides.

Roman games and entertainments

Roman games and entertainments often seem surprisingly modern. Visitors to museums are often surprised to find that the Romans had board games and played games with bats and balls.

● The list below includes a number of objects which have been found in different parts of Britain. Arrange the finds in this list into five groups : TOYS, CHILDREN'S GAMES, HUNTING, GLADIATORS, OTHER ENTERTAINMENTS.

— carved model of a bear (Essex);
— hunting scene on a bowl (Northamptonshire);
— bronze model of a gladiator (London);
— board game with counters (Silchester);
— leather bikini worn by a girl acrobat (London);
— dice (London);
— bone flute (London);
— mosaic of gladiators fighting (Sussex);
— clay mould of a hockey player with a curved stick and a ball (Northamptonshire);
— toy men (Essex);
— a mosaic showing a hunting scene (Somerset);
— gladiator's helmet (Suffolk);
— iron trident (London);
— mosaic of a man holding a hare (Gloucestershire);
— carving of a goddess holding a riding whip used for hunting (Avon).

Roman theatre at St Albans, Hertfordshire

Mosaics showing different entertainments in a Roman amphitheatre

Index

First published in Great Britain 1984
by Hulton Educational Publications Ltd
Raans Road, Amersham, Bucks HP6 6JJ

Text © Philip A. Sauvain 1984
Illustrations © Hulton Educational Publications Ltd 1984

ISBN 0 7175 1237 1

Phototypesetting by Oxford Publishing Services, Oxford
Printed in Hong Kong by Wing King Tong Co. Ltd

Acknowledgements

The author and publishers are grateful to the following for permission to reproduce the photographs on the pages listed.

Aerofilms Ltd, 30L, 63L; British Tourist Authority, 24; City and County Museum, Lincoln, 62; Committee for Aerial Photography, University of Cambridge, 37, 44; Robert Harding Associates, 14L; Mansell Collection, 16R, 17, 38; Danish National Museum, Copenhagen, 60; Trustees of the British Museum, 10T, 14R, 48 (Crown Copyright Reserved); Trustees of the Museum of London, 33; Verulamium Museum, St Albans, 54; Roger Wood, 63R

All other photographs supplied by the author.

Artwork by David Bryant, Barry Gurbutt and Jeff Edwards
Edited and designed by Ela Ginalska